W9-AFB-346

POLITICAL REALITIES
Edited on behalf of the Politics Association by
Derek Heater

Government and Politics of Northern Ireland

Second Edition

Paul Arthur

Longman
London and New York

LONGMAN GROUP LIMITED
Longman House
Burnt Mill, Harlow, Essex

First published 1980
Second Edition 1984
ISBN 0 582 35480 3

*Computer typeset by SB Datagraphics,
printed and bound by Spottiswoode Ballantyne,
Colchester and London*

British Library Cataloguing in Publication Data

Arthur, Paul, 1945–
   Government and Politics of Northern
   Ireland.—2nd ed.—(Political realities)
   1. Northern Ireland—Politics and government
   I. Title   II. Series
   320.9416   JN1572.A2

   ISBN 0-582-35480-3

Library of Congress Cataloging in Publication Data

Arthur, Paul, 1945–
   Government and Politics of Northern Ireland.

   (Political realities)
   Bibliography: p.
   Includes index.
   1. Northern Ireland—Politics and government.
   I. Title.   II. Series.
   JN1572.A2A77 1984   320.9416   83-26803
   ISBN 0-582-35480-3

Contents

Political Realities:
the nature of the series

A great need is felt for short books which can supplement or even replace textbooks and which can deal in an objective but realistic way with problems that arouse political controversy. The series aims to break from a purely descriptive and institutional approach to one that will show how and why there are different interpretations both of how things work and how they ought to work. Too often in the past 'British Constitution' has been taught quite apart from any knowledge of the actual political conflicts which institutions strive to contain. So the Politics Association sponsors this new series because it believes that a specifically civic education is an essential part of any liberal or general education, but that respect for political rules and an active citizenship can only be encouraged by helping pupils, students and young voters to discover what the main objects are of political controversy, the varying views about the nature of the constitution – themselves often highly political – and what the most widely canvassed alternative policies are in their society. From such a realistic appreciation of differences and conflicts reasoning can then follow about the common processes of containing or resolving them peacefully.

The specific topics chosen are based on an analysis of the main elements in existing A level syllabuses, and the manner in which they are treated is based on the conviction of the editors that almost every examination board is moving, slowly but surely, away from a concentration on constitutional rules and towards a more difficult but important concept of a realistic political education or the enhancement of political literacy.

This approach has, of course, been common enough in the universities for many years. Quite apart from its civic importance, the teaching of politics in schools has tended to lag behind university practice and expectations. So the editors have aimed to draw on the most up-to-date academic knowledge, with some of the books being written by university teachers, some by secondary or further education teachers, but each aware of the skills and knowledge of the other.

The Politics Association and the editors are conscious of the great importance of other levels of education, and are actively pursuing studies and projects of curriculum development in several directions, particularly towards CSE needs; but it was decided to begin with A level and new developments in sixth form courses precisely because of the great overlap here between teaching in secondary school and further education colleges, whether specifically for examinations or not; indeed most of the books will be equally useful for general studies.

Bernard Crick
Derek Heater

Preface to the Second Edition

This new edition extends the narrative to May 1984. It is somewhat less tentative than the earlier edition because it maintains yet again that 'objectivity' is not an emotive vacuum. There can have been very few people who have lived through these past fifteen years unscathed by the violence. The near future is not bright so it behoves us not to succumb to despair. For that reason I draw readers' attention to the actors outside the province. They have a positive role to play, and that is the theme of my concluding remarks.

The bulk of new material is contained in the final two chapters. Earlier changes are in response to corrections noted by Denis Norman and T. K. Daniel. I thank them for their assistance.

Paul Arthur
Ulster Polytechnic, May 1984

Preface

> ... the emotive neutrality which should characterize the chronicler is
> not the same thing as indifference, and his objectivity can only be the
> result of a subjective passion for the pursuit of truth. It is a poor sort of
> impartiality which stands outside the parties untouched by their
> emotions; the good judge, like the playwright and historian, absorbs the
> subjective truth contained in each of the conflicting pleas, and his
> verdict is a synthesis of their part-truths, not their denial. In other
> words, "objectivity" is a state of balanced emotions, not an emotive
> vacuum.
>
> Arthur Koestler, *Promise and Fulfilment. Palestine 1917–49*
> (London, 1949) p. viii

This book strives to be an 'objective' (in Koestler's sense of the word)
account of political life in Northern Ireland since 1921. The reader
will soon be aware that virtually any political event in Ulster can be
invested with at least two interpretations. Readers must judge for
themselves the measure of 'objectivity' which has been reached. I
hope they will agree that it is not a 'neutral' book, and insofar as they
do disagree with my opinions they will be sufficiently stimulated to
continue their readings further.

Of course, it is not simply a book about opinions. The bulk of the
text attempts to convey as comprehensively as possible the mechanics
of politics and administration in Northern Ireland over a period of
about sixty years. In such a short book omissions have been
inevitable. I hope that none of these are too grave.

In preparing this for publication I have received valuable
assistance from many people. Friends in the Ulster Polytechnic who
have been helpful include Steve Payne, Henry Patterson, Paul Bew,
T. K. Daniel and Denis Norman. Professor A. J. A. Morris has
given me every possible facility to complete the manuscript.
Particular thanks are due to the Series editors, Professor Bernard
Crick and Derek Heater, who have offered me helpful advice,
courteous attention and incredible patience. None of these people
can be held responsible for any of my shortcomings.

Paul Arthur

List of Abbreviations

No political connotation is intended by the use of the following: 'Ulster', 'the North', 'the province' for 'Northern Ireland'; 'Derry' for 'Londonderry'; 'the South' for 'the Republic of Ireland'. The terms 'Catholic' and 'Protestant' have been used solely for community identification.

AOH	Ancient Order of Hibernians
BBC	British Broadcasting Corporation
DUP	Democratic Unionist Party
EEC	European Economic Community
GOCNI	General Officer Commanding, Northern Ireland
IIP	**Irish Independence Party**
IRA	Irish Republican Army
ITA	Independent Television Authority
NICRA	Northern Ireland Civil Rights Association
NILP	Northern Ireland Labour Party
PR	Proportional Representation
PSF	**Provisional Sinn Fein**
RUC	Royal Ulster Constabulary
SDLP	Social Democratic and Labour Party
UCDC	Ulster Constitution Defence Committee
UDA	Ulster Defence Association
UDR	Ulster Defence Regiment
ULDP	**Ulster Loyalist Democratic Party**
UPNI	Unionist Party of Northern Ireland
UUC	Ulster Unionist Council
UUUP	**United Ulster Unionist Party**
UVF	Ulster Volunteer Force
UWC	Ulster Workers' Council
VUP	Vanguard Unionist Party
WP	**Workers' Party**

Ireland

1 The Genesis of the Ulster Crisis: Themes and Myths

> The story of the plantation of Ulster is underwritten by the hand of Almighty God.
>
> Clifford Smyth[1]

> We pursue her [England] like a sleuth-hound; we lie in wait for her and come upon her like a thief in the night; and some day we will overwhelm her with the wrath of God . . . It is not that we are apostles of hate. Who like us has carried Christ's word of charity about the earth?
>
> Patrick Pearse[2]

> For the most part, the myth-maker does not invent his facts; he interprets facts that are already given in the culture to which he belongs. What marks his account as being a myth is, not its content, but its dramatic form and the fact that it serves as a practical argument.
>
> Henry Tudor[3]

The Ulster plantation

England's domination of Ireland began with the Anglo-Norman invasion of 1169, although the conquest of the island did not begin in earnest until the Tudors came to power. When Henry VIII became King of Ireland in 1541 he bequeathed two of the lasting problems of Anglo-Irish relations – religion and land – by attempting to impose Protestantism on Gaelic Catholics and by confiscating land on a huge scale.

It was the plantation of Ulster begun in 1607 by new Protestant settlers which properly cemented English rule in Ireland. Ulster was a special prize. Her warriors had a proud tradition having been engaged in endemic warfare with the 'men of Ireland' since early Celtic times. They had successfully held off Elizabethan troops long after the rest of Ireland had succumbed, and it was not until 1603 that they were defeated by a vastly superior military force. With 'the flight of the Earls' (Ulster's leaders, O'Neill and O'Donnell, who had been unable to settle down under the new regime) in 1607, the way was now open for the plantation to be undertaken.

The plantation succeeded because its conception had been 'strategic and scientific'. It entailed the building of 23 new towns to protect the material needs of the settlers. It 'was the most important scheme for the building of towns to be carried out in the British Isles before the end of the Second World War'[4]: Their great numbers, 170,000 in all, allowed for self-sufficiency and ensured that they need not mix with the native Irish. By 1703 Catholics owned less than 14 per cent of the land.

Most important was the fact that 150,000 of them came from lowland Scotland, renewing the historic link between Ulster and Scotland: 'Throughout human times this northern province, and particularly the two counties of Antrim and Down which were and are at its core and from which it took the name Ulidia, has had intimate relations with Scotland. The distinctive personality of Ulster is of course older than partition, but it is also far older than the Protestant plantation of the seventeenth century. . . .'[5]

Religion separated planter and Gael. The Scots were Presbyterians deeply suspicious of Stuart flirtations with 'Popery'. They brought with them their own set of customs relating to landholdings which were diffused throughout the entire Protestant community. This 'Ulster tenant right' created an atmosphere of greater social and political stability and encouraged continuous economic growth and risk taking. Great emphasis was placed on education, self-discipline and shrewd financial dealings. It encouraged rapid capital accumulation which sowed the seeds of Ulster's nineteenth-century industrial revolution, an event which was to set it off from the rest of Ireland.

The plantation's success was not secured until 1690 when the Protestant forces of William of Orange defeated the Catholics led by James II. The spirit of the seventeenth century was one of unmitigated settler-native hostility. The native response to the plantation was the Ulster Rebellion of 1641 when thousands of Protestants were murdered or driven from their holdings. Protestant revenge was wreaked by the excesses of Cromwellian troops later in the decade and finally by William's victory at the Boyne in 1690.

The Ulster plantation has had a profound significance in Anglo-Irish history. In the short term, all of Ireland was now firmly incorporated in the periphery of English politics and administration.

The planters, representing a strident reformed religion, were both contemptuous and fearful of the indigenous religion. Assimilation became impossible, and a fundamental religio-political division was created. Even today a prominent Unionist politician can assert: 'It is not political partition only that is in Ireland. It is a fundamental partition. It is that between people and people, between the open Bible and pure evangelical faith, and a power that would draw back again into a dense darkness from which there has been a merciful deliverance.'[6]

Geographical proximity, deep historical links, a shared language and customs all supported the thesis that the plantation was a sort of home-coming. The twin problems of religion and national identity combined to create the intractable Ulster question. Whether we view the plantation in biblical terms as a return of the Celtic people of Scotland reinvigorated with the reformed faith, or as an example of naked colonisation and exploitation, we cannot ignore its powers for myth-making. To this day its symbolism is evoked by Unionist leaders at political meetings.

But that is not to say that the faithful will not be shielded from umpleasant facts: take, for example, the portrait entitled 'The entry of King William into Ireland' by the Dutch court painter, Pieter van der Meulen. In acknowledging the fact that William fought at the Boyne with the blessing of Pope Innocent XI (intent on halting the progress of Louis XIV and his ally James II) the artist depicted William and the Pope in the same portrait. In 1933 when it was hung in the new Northern Ireland Parliament at Stormont, there were instant complaints and it was removed only after a preacher came across from Scotland and slashed the blasphemous picture. The battle of the Boyne was not to be seen against a European backcloth of 'high politics'; its purpose was to symbolise the triumph of Protestantism and the plantation in Ulster.

The '98

> ... these men aimed at nothing less than a social and political revolution such as had been accomplished in France ... Nothing less would have succeeded in causing Protestant and Catholic masses to shake hands over the bloody chasm of religious hatreds, nothing less will accomplish the same result in our day among the Irish workers.[7]

Religious tension also existed within the Protestant communion. The Episcopalian (Anglican) Establishment opposed every force throughout the British Isles which challenged the absolute authority of the Crown in civil and ecclesiastical life. As early as 1636 some Presbyterians attempted to emigrate to New England from Belfast. One observer has calculated that by the time of the American Revolution there were perhaps 200,000 'Ulster-Scots' there. Influenced by the radical and democratic ideas in vogue and embittered by their own experience in the British Isles, they fought against the Crown forces.

In common with Catholics they were compelled to pay tithes to the Established (Episcopalian) Church and were deprived of effective participation in the political life of the Kingdom. They wanted to win independence for the Irish parliament (Grattan's Parliament 1782–1800) and make it a genuine representative assembly instead of the preserve of a corrupt ascendancy. Throughout the eighteenth century they suffered most of the civil and religious disabilities imposed on the Catholics. Given this sense of shared grievance a temporary alliance developed. A body known as the United Irishmen was founded in Belfast in 1791 by middle-class radicals, largely Presbyterians, with the object of uniting 'the whole people of Ireland, to abolish the memory of all past dissensions, and to substitute the common name of Irishman in place of the denominations of Protestant, Catholic and dissenter'.

Their greatest achievement was the contribution they made to the passing of the Catholic Relief Act of 1793 which conceded parliamentary franchise to Catholics on equal terms with Protestants without allowing them to sit in parliament. But their more impatient souls were not prepared to work within a constitutional framework. Their opportunity came in 1798: England had quelled a naval mutiny and was becoming conscious of a growing French threat. The '98 was an embarrassing failure, being confined largely to three counties. In Antrim and Down Presbyterian radicals took up arms but the Catholic population remained quiescent. Eighteen (out of 183) ministers in the Ulster Synod were involved, and of these ten were imprisoned and two executed. In the southern county of Wexford a Catholic populist uprising succeeded in killing some Protestants.

The non-sectarian alliance was at an end. The steady erosion of the Penal Laws towards the end of the eighteenth century had removed its chief prop. The disbandment of Grattan's Parliament in 1800 and the total integration of Ireland within British political institutions by the Act of Union (1800) were further reasons for the drift between Catholic and Dissenter. Another abortive rising (by Robert Emmet in 1803) heightened the siege mentality of *all* Protestants in Ireland. A Presbyterian and former United Irish sympathiser records being frightened by a singing procession of Catholics: 'I begin to fear these people and think, like the Jews, they will regain their native land.'[8]

As a military exercise the '98 was a failure, but it serves as a powerful myth. Twentieth-century Republicans hold it as a central tenet of their belief that a non-sectarian working-class alliance is not only possible but inevitable as soon as Protestant workers divest themselves of those political leaders who have duped them for selfish economic reasons. To sustain this belief a hagiography of Protestant Home Rule leaders and movements is drawn up: the leadership of Isaac Butt and Parnell in the nineteenth century; Sir Roger Casement's role in the 1916 Rising; the ministerial post accepted by Ernest Blythe, a northern Protestant, in the first government of the Irish Free State; the temporary alliance of Belfast's unemployed in 1932; and the appearance of an IRA contingent from Belfast's Shankill Road at Bodenstown (the graveyard of Wolfe Tone, founder of the United Irishmen) in 1934.

Two nations?

There are two national communities in Ireland: the Ulster Protestant community and the Catholic community. . . .[9]

A common explanation for the partition of the island in 1921 lies in the uneven development of Irish capitalism. This refers to the fact that a modern industrial capitalism developed in Ulster in the course of the nineteenth century, while in the south the mixed economy of comparatively large industries and agriculture declined. That capitalism did develop in the Greater Belfast area is beyond dispute. (Her population increase from 37,000 in 1821 to 208,000 in 1881 is but one indicator.) Her access to Imperial markets and raw materials made it inevitable that she would resist proposals for a united Home Rule Ireland which might at some future date set up a protective tariff wall around Ireland. Thus, in the Home Rule crises in the years after 1886, Ulster's apologists sought to emphasise the distinction between her and the rest of Ireland by adopting a 'two nations' thesis. Meanwhile Irish nationalists were missing the significance of Belfast's phenomenal growth.

Rural Ireland resented being placed at the mercy of the legislature of industrial Britain where disinterest rather than deliberate malice permitted great suffering and injustice. Peel's Commission of 1843 to inquire into Irish agrarian problems remarked upon 'the patient endurance which the labouring classes have generally exhibited under sufferings greater, we believe, than the people of any other country in Europe have to sustain'. That suffering was compounded by successive failures of the potato crop in the mid 1840s. The Great Famine left one million dead and forced another million to emigrate. Many emigrants were convinced that Britain had not done enough to avert the disaster or alleviate the misery. Some formed the Irish Republican Brotherhood, the prototype of violent nationalism, in the United States. Those who remained joined Michael Davitt's Land League in the great land agitation of 1879–82 in a bid to achieve peasant proprietorships. State-aided land purchase became possible from 1885.

Owing to its mixed economy Ulster avoided the ravages of the Famine; a smaller proportion of the rural population were dependent on the potato as its staple diet. And Ulster avoided the excesses of the Land War too. Its landlords displayed an exceptional sensitivity to the demands of their tenant farmers because they saw the Land League as a threat to British power in Ireland. Thus the northern tenantry were the passive beneficiaries of the southern Land League. They accepted the strategy of 'a more excellent way': 'As the Unionists were prepared to produce an accommodation on the land question, there was no need for the tenant farmers to break with the staunch honest community of Ulster Protestantism by joining in the "dishonest" methods of the "violent" and "unruly" southern tenantry.'[10] So Gladstone's ploy of linking his Home Rule Bill with a generous land bill in an attempt to split the Unionist bloc by activating landlord/tenant conflict in Ulster failed. The Ulster farmer had a political and ideological commitment to the Union.

The Belfast working class had an even greater economic interest in maintaining the Union:

The Liberal-Unionist case against Home Rule, adumbrated by Thomas Sinclair with increasing cogency from 1886, was quite simply that *Belfast* had done very well under the Union: her population had quadrupled in fifty years, her wage rates were higher than anywhere in Ireland and in some cases up to British standards; as to customs revenue she ranked as the third port in the United Kingdom, being exceeded only by London and Liverpool; she had the largest weaving factory, the largest shipping output, the largest tobacco factory, and the largest ropeworks in the world. The basis of her prosperity was the economic link with Britain, and she was not prepared to come under the rule of a Dublin Parliament dominated by impoverished small farmers from Munster and Connaught.[11]

While Ulster's population soared, that in the southern provinces went into decline; while its tenant farmers garnered the spoils of the Land War painlessly, the southern peasant proprietors inherited an agricultural system which was impoverished and underproductive; and while its industrialisation accentuated Ulster's distinctiveness within Ireland, southern industry had been in decline since the end of the eighteenth century. The 'two nations' thesis, originally put forward in 1896, had been influenced by Disraeli's use of the term in an English context. When the question of partition was to arise thirty years later the 'two nations' concept took on a more polemical hue. It is still with us today as a loyalist apologia for, if not union with Britain, then permanent separation from the Irish Republic.

'Home Rule Means Rome Rule': the rise of majoritarianism

... there is a ragged little urchin selling newspapers, and crying every morning the *Morning News*. That ragged urchin under the new code is to be Marquis of Donegal. There is a Nationalist rivetter on Queen's Island, and he is to be successor to W. J. Pirrie ... and Paddy O'Rafferty, a ragman, resident in the slums of Smithfield, is to succeed Sir Edward Harland as the next mayor of Belfast ...[12]

The above is an extract from a speech made at an anti-Home Rule meeting in Belfast in January 1886. Its elemental bigotry demonstrates Protestant defensiveness at a time of growing unemployment, and in anticipation at the passing of the Home Rule Bill. The Catholic population of Belfast had risen sharply during the nineteenth century and had reached a peak of 34 per cent in 1861. Thereafter it began to decline. In a society where there was fierce competition for jobs Catholics represented a threat.

Nationally Catholic self-confidence had grown. The passing of the Catholic Emancipation Act in 1829 opened the way for Catholics to assert themselves in public life. An endowment to the Catholic seminary at Maynooth in 1845 undermined Protestant confidence in the government. Most importantly, the disestablishment of the Church of Ireland in 1869 removed one of the major props which underpinned the Act of Union. The Orange Order Grand Lodge even passed a resolution making it no longer an obligation of membership that a member support the Union.

During these years mass democracy in Britain emerged. The last vestiges of wholesale corruption in political life were removed with the passing of the Reform Acts of 1867 and 1884, the Ballot Act (1872), the Corrupt Practices Act (1883), and the Redistribution of Seats Act (1885). Charles Stewart Parnell, leader of the Irish nationalists, realised the significance of this constitutional revolution, and soon moulded a disciplined party machine to the nationalist cause. When his party won the overwhelming bulk of Irish seats in the 1885 general election, including a majority of one in 'loyal' Ulster, any hope of political dialogue disappeared. Political Protestantism had been caught off guard and must organise to ensure that this did not happen again; Catholic nationalism had demonstrated that it had a clear majority throughout the whole of the island:

> The results of the arrival of political mass democracy, in the last third of the nineteenth century, made it hard to keep up the pretence that the [religio/political] division had been exaggerated ... The Catholics were, after all, in a large majority in the whole island when they voted en bloc, as they were now doing. And a majority was what mass democracy was about .. The minority had the right to vote against but after that it should do like other minorities and accept the majority decision.[13]

Protestant fears were very real. They began to detect the growth of a Catholic monolith:

> After the collapse of the Gladstone government over the Irish universities Bill and the refusal to allow denominationalism of Irish education, the Church no longer tried to support political

liberalism in Ireland. At the cost of great simplification we can say that, whereas before 1873 the Church tried to advance its interests within the Imperial UK situation, after 1873 it changed its attitude, working on the assumption that a satisfactory solution to the educational question could not be found except in the context of a self-governing Ireland.[14]

By 1882 Parnell was calling on the Catholic clergy to play a more active role in his National League. The influence of clericalism became so pronounced that in the years after 1896 Belfast branches of the National League were dissolved and replaced by a Catholic Association run by Bishop Henry.

Protestantism was conscious of its own disunity. The '98 had graphically demonstrated the 'basic confessional antagonism within the Protestant population: the United Irishmen wholly Presbyterian, the Orangemen wholly Episcopalian; intrinsically "democratic" Presbyterian, intrinsically "deferential" Episcopalians'.[15] Presbyterians were not officially admitted into the Orange Order until 1834. The Episcopalians consistently opposed Home Rule measures, and Ulster's five bishops even supported the unionist case which went close to treason in 1912. Yet the official historian of the Presbyterian Church in Ireland records that Presbyterianism did not swing against Home Rule until 1909 when the *Ne Temere* decree (which insisted that the children of a mixed marriage be brought up as Catholics) was introduced. Before that date Presbyterians had been almost equally divided on the question, but now they feared a 'new ascendancy' in which the Roman Church would be in a position to deny the validity of their marriages and the legitimacy of their children.

But we must not exaggerate Protestant interdenominational conflict. The political nature of Protestantism altered in the nineteenth century. In the early decades a long debate had gone on within Presbyterianism between the adherents of the New Light or liberal wing, and those of the Old Light, the authoritarian conservatives who allowed no flexibility in creed or in interpretation. The Old Light victory in 1829 diminished the liberal stain in Presbyterianism. The first major sectarian riot seems to have occurred in 1835 and was repeated at least once a decade until the close of the century. By 1857 the *Belfast Newsletter* was publishing articles on 'Romish intolerance'.

It is worthwhile noting the extent to which Ulster was part of an international religious phenomenon during this period. The beginning of the century had been 'an era of relatively good feelings' in religiously heterogeneous countries,[16] but by mid-century relations had worsened: Switzerland's Sonderbund War (1847) was fought between Catholic and Protestant cantons; Germans endured the Kulturkampf; and certain British and North American cities experienced sectarian riots between 1830–70. Large-scale movements of population within countries and between continents was one factor encouraging sectarianism; contiguity reinforced sectarianism. Internationally, a proselytising evangelical Protestantism reacted against Catholicism's ultramontane movement and, paradoxically, the rise of nationalism failed to blur religious differences in Switzerland and Germany.

To counter the twin threat of Catholicism and nationalism Ulster loyalists began to organise. The Orange Order – founded in 1795 as an Episcopalian peasant self-defence grouping – served to weaken the basic confessional antagonism within Protestantism. Its rapid growth in Belfast from 1,335 members in 1851 to 4,000 in 1870 underlined the nature of Protestant fears. Long before the 1885 electoral debacle, an Orange leader anticipated its role as Protestantism's reply to the Catholic monolith:

> ... Popery is something more than a religious system: it is a political system also. It is a religio-political system for the enslavement of the body and soul of man and it cannot be met by any mere religious system or by any mere political system. It must be opposed by such a combination as the Orange Society, based upon religion and carrying over religion into the politics of the day.[17]

By the 1880s the age of the machine politician had arrived. Parnell saw its significance in 1885; and by 1905 Protestant homogeneity was secured in the founding of the Ulster Unionist Council. The simplistic notion that majoritarianism equalled democracy became the bane of any sensible political dialogue in Ireland. Both factions used it with a religious zeal, for to pursue a policy of conciliation meant conceding the existence of two communities, and by recognising the separate existence of a minority community almost inevitably encouraged the heightening of its claim.

The Ulster question at Westminster

> ... these foul Ulster Tories have always ruined our party.
>
> Lord Randolph Churchill, 1886

In January 1886 Gladstone formed a Government dependent on the Parnellite vote. In April he introduced a Home Rule Bill to restore a parliament and independent executive to Ireland with authority over all matters except defence, foreign policy, trade and navigation. Expediency was not simply his motive; he had recognised Irish nationalist demands as early as 1845. Many Liberals did not share his convictions. Notwithstanding vague promises to the Protestant minority, Nonconformists feared for their safety, while the Radicals in this age of the 'new imperialism' saw Irish demands as a threat to the Empire. Moreover, the Irish party, which had been obstructing parliamentary business intermittently since 1874, was not popular in the House.

Randolph Churchill astutely played the 'Orange card' in 1886. He combined expediency – he was attempting to capture the Tory leadership from below – with principle (the Bill would plunge the knife into 'the heart of the Empire'). The Bill was defeated in June with 93 Liberals voting against it. The same fate awaited the second Home Rule Bill in 1892. That appeared to be the end of the matter. With the exception of 1892–95 the Conservatives were in power from 1886–1906. The Parnellites were deeply divided as a result of the controversy surrounding their leader's extra-marital adventure, and the Liberals appeared to be a spent force.

But all that presupposes that only the Irish Question exercised the minds of Westminster politicians. In fact the Social Question allowed the Liberals another term of office following their massive victory in 1906 on a manifesto of radical social reform. It was the rejection of the People's Budget by the Lords in November 1909 which occasioned a grave constitutional crisis and reintroduced the Irish Question. Lloyd George wanted to curtail the Lords' veto power on legislation. An appeal to the country solved little, and in another general election (December 1910) the Irish Nationalists were left holding the balance of power. With the passing of the Parliament Act in 1911 the Liberals were able to pay their debt by introducing a third Home Rule Bill in 1912.

Ulster was prepared. It had already adopted some of the tactics of its nationalist opponents. Mass meetings in 1892, 1911 and 1912 preceded the signing of the Ulster Covenant by 471,414 persons on 28 September 1912. The Covenant, modelled on the Scottish League and Covenant originally drawn up in 1580, committed Ulster to the Union and loyalty to the Crown. Its signing was a piece of politics-as-theatre, beginning with meetings in the west of the province and sweeping in towards Belfast. Its cathartic effect has been noted:

> ... the Ulster Covenant with its ceremonial and promise of inflexible readiness to resist by violence if necessary, and with its solemn stylistic derivation from Protestant tradition, was in fact a brilliant means of enabling Unionist sentiment to demonstrate its force and give itself a sense of liberation while diverting itself into channels which would offset the psychological need for anti-Catholic riot.[18]

The organisation of gun-running into Ulster ports in September 1912, the formation of the paramilitary Ulster Volunteer Force (UVF), and the approval of the establishment of a provisional government if Home Rule was ever introduced, all pointed to Unionist strategy and conviction. They, too, could resort to violence or the threat of violence. (This uneasy alliance of constitutionalism and putative violence was to be a feature of party politics in Ulster after partition in 1921.)

Perhaps a surprising feature of these events was total Conservative acquiesence in this 'semi-constitutional' activity. There was tremendous emotional satisfaction in fighting the Ulster cause. Their leader, Bonar Law, had close family ties with Ulster. His assertion, 'I can imagine no length of resistance to which Ulster can go in which I should not be prepared to support them', reflected his own commitment. His party believed itself to be protecting the Protestant minority. More significantly, it was recontesting the Parliament Act which it saw as a conspiracy between the Liberals and the Nationalists. In Britain the Union Defence League collected nearly two million signatures for its Covenant pledging 'any action that may be effective in preventing it (Home Rule) being put into operation, and more particularly to prevent the armed forces of the Crown being used to deprive the people of Ulster of their rights as citizens of the United Kingdom'. Signatories included Lords Balfour of Burleigh, Milner and Roberts, Viscount Halifax, Admiral of the Fleet Sir E.

Seymour, Rudyard Kipling, Sir Edward Elgar and Professor A. V. Dicey. The Army establishment lent their support: Sir Henry Wilson assisted the UVF; and officers at the Curragh camp refused to mobilise their men lest they be moved against Ulster loyalists in March 1914. This remarkable reaction has been described thus: 'No stranger episode is to be found in the history of conservatism than its abandonment of all pretensions in the three years before the First World War to be the party of "law and order". For this Bonar Law carried his full share of responsibility, not least because of his indifference to the existence of that nice distinction which divides conservatism from reaction.'[19]

The Bill completed the journey in May 1914 after the Lords had used its full powers of delay. It became necessary to insert two important provisos in the 1914 Home Rule Act: it was not to come into operation until the war had ended; and amending legislation would be necessary to make special provision for Ulster. At Westminster deep divisions had been created. In the long term Britain's interests may have been more seriously affected, since the Irish Question dominated parliamentary life during the period when Britain should have been mobilising her resources in preparation for the First World War.

Political conditions altered during the war. A coalition government, heavily dependent on Tory support after the 1918 election, came into office. John Redmond, leader of the Irish party at Westminster, committed 160,000 of his followers to the war effort, and won many allies in Britain. But his party suffered. In 1916 republicans staged an uprising in Dublin. It went the way of previous rebellions, short and bloody but raising the ghosts of romantic Ireland. Government over-reaction made martyrs of the rebels. As a result the Irish Parliamentary Party was decimated in the 1918 election. Violent republicanism now claimed to speak for the vast majority of Irish people. Right was on her side: 'The Anglo-Irish conflict of 1912–22 took place when a great positive force supported independence movements. The emergence of new, or "reborn" ethnic states was a feature of the history of the time, the culmination of powerful ideas cultivated in the western world throughout the nineteenth century.'[20] A bitter Anglo-Irish battle was waged after 1918. Eventually the British public conscience revolted. A solution would have to be found.

In Ulster the idea of partition as a solution first emerged publicly in 1916. Previously the loyalists had used the Ulster question to block Home Rule rather than attempt the more limited goal of winning concessions for Ulster's Protestants. One of their two outstanding leaders, Sir Edward Carson, a Tory Cabinet member and Dublin lawyer with considerable forensic skills and organisational ability, was decidedly not an Ulster Unionist. He was a man who 'did not care for the Northern Orangemen, ... their speeches, he said reminded him of "the unrolling of a mummy – all old bones and rotten rags"'.[21] He was fighting for the Union of 1800, and when it was destroyed he retired from the fray.

A clumsy attempt by Lloyd George to gather together all the interested parties and produce a watered-down version of Home Rule failed in the Irish Convention of 1917. Now the problem for Unionism was to decide the boundaries of Ulster. The most obvious division was to separate off Ulster's nine counties from the rest of the country. But Walter Long reported to the Cabinet Committee on Ireland on 3 February 1920 that, '... the people in the inner circles hold the view that the new province should consist of the six counties, the idea being that the inclusion of Donegal, Cavan and Monaghan would provide such an access of strength to the Roman Catholic party, that the supremacy of the Unionists would be seriously threatened'.

For that reason three counties were sacrificed at the altar of majoritarianism and not simply a transient majority but an overwhelming one that was artificially stimulated. Besides, the Unionists were accepting the logic of the Ulster Plantation which had 'held' mainly in the north-east, and of the Industrial Revolution which was a product of the Greater Belfast area.

The Ulster Unionists adopted a note of self-sacrificing patriotism when Lloyd George exercised a form of moral blackmail accusing them of weakening the war effort – and thus the Empire – by their intransigence. They were prepared to accept the new Home Rule Bill introduced in 1919 and enacted in 1920 . . . 'Much against our wishes but in the interests of peace we accepted this as a final settlement . . .' (Sir James Craig to Lloyd George, July 1921). The Government of Ireland Act which became law on 23 December 1920 and became operative in June 1921, partitioned Ireland.

The imperial power considered it a satisfactory settlement: 'The two supreme services which Ireland has rendered Britain are her accession to the Allied cause on the outbreak of the Great War, and her withdrawal from the House of Commons at its close.'[22] The loyalists, if left in peace, would present no more problems for Britain: and Catholic Ireland in the Irish Free State was embroiled in a civil war over the terms of the agreement signed with Britain.

Conclusion

Like all other myths, a political myth explains the circumstances of those to whom it is addressed. It renders their experience more coherent; it helps them understand the world in which they live. And it does so by enabling them to see their present condition as an episode in an ongoing drama ... and, as often as not, it identifies the enemy of the group and promises eventual victory. It offers, in short an account of the past and the future in the light of which the present can be understood. And as we would expect, this account is, not only an explanation, but also a practical argument.[23]

The Irish are not peculiar in possessing political myths, but they are unfortunate in having opposing sets of myths. Remembering 1690 and the men of '98 are not simple folk memories; rather they are ideological weapons to be brandished before every generation. History is about a practical argument; who's in and who's out, who wins and who loses, are at the centre of an ongoing drama. Partition in 1921 merely closed a scene; the ghosts of history could be evoked yet again before the opening of the next act.

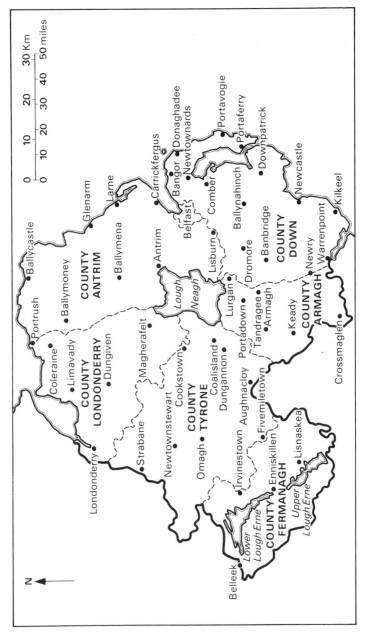

Northern Ireland – the Six Counties

2 A 'Decorative' Constitution

The most important characteristic of a constitution . . . is the extent to which it is obeyed; and the distinction between regulative and decorative constitutions is of greater importance than the classifications of constitutional jurisprudence. Conversely, we could classify politics according to the degree of constitutional hypocrisy – that is to say, the discrepancy between proclaimed principles and practice.

Stanislav Andreski[1]

But because we are a country with no real history of constitution-making we may underrate the importance of constitutional forms elsewhere. In the rest of the world, constitutional devices do play a part in shaping the governmental process. These devices, moreover, reflect political ideas. The study of constitutions is then one of the best ways of linking the study of theories and institutions.

F. F. Ridley[2]

What does a British politician do when he finds himself responsible for a social order divided by fundamental conflict? He writes a new political constitution for it. . . . The illusions of constitutionalism have great staying power among those who never have to pay the costs of their own illusions.

Alisdair MacIntyre[3]

Political background

During the debate on the Second Reading of the 1920 Bill the Chancellor of the Exchequer wondered 'whether I shall be too sanguine if I express the hope that this may be the last of a great series of historic debates on proposals for the better government of Ireland'.[4] Events were to undermine his hopes. The majority of Irishmen preferred self-government to better government; and those that resisted were to be coerced into obedience. Partition of the island seemed the only solution to the conflicting demands of Unionist and Nationalist.

During that period the Cabinet had three concerns – Cabinet unity, Imperial unity and the defence of Britain. A Liberal, Lloyd George, led a Cabinet containing a number of English Unionists; he had to ensure that they were not split on the Irish issue. He had also to maintain the integrity of the Empire and was afraid that Ireland might set a precedent for the other dominions – if it fell by the wayside, others might follow. Finally Britain recognised the need to protect her flank and to secure the Atlantic seaboard; hence she insisted on retaining certain Irish ports for the protection of sea-routes. So both pragmatism *and* principle came into play in seeking out an Anglo-Irish solution.

Divided counsels dictated events in southern Ireland. The territory was at war with Britain from 1919 until the signature of the Anglo-Irish Treaty on 6 December 1921. The Treaty established a self-governing dominion under the title of the Irish Free State for the whole island. By presenting an Address to the Crown, Northern Ireland could retain its status under the 1920 Act; this option was exercised immediately. The Parliament of Southern Ireland assembled on 14 January 1922. Partition had become a reality.

The Irish Free State was born into civil war. The Treaty signatories, led by Michael Collins, believed that they had won 'the freedom to achieve freedom'. They felt that a Belfast parliament would not be financially viable and that the territory it controlled would be diminished considerably by a proposed Boundary Commission. The anti-Treatyites, led by Eamonn De Valera, believed in the myth of the 'indivisible island'. The Treaty represented betrayal and the Belfast parliament another example of English perfidy. After attempts at agreement had failed the Civil War broke out on 28 June 1922.

The boundary between Northern Ireland and the Irish Free State was settled in 1925. The Council of Ireland was formally dissolved in 1926 and those parts of the 1920 Act which referred to the Irish Free State were repealed at Westminster in 1927. Thereafter relations between Belfast and Dublin moved further apart. By the External Relations Act 1936, the Irish Free State removed all mention of the Crown from its constitution. In 1937 a new Irish Constitution was adopted. It applied in theory to the whole of Ireland but jurisdiction was limited to the 26 counties, now to be known as Eire, 'pending the re-integration of the national territory'. Finally, on Easter Day 1949,

Eire formally became the Republic of Ireland, following the passing of the Republic of Ireland Act 1948, and left the Commonwealth.

As a consequence the Westminster Parliament passed the Ireland Act 1949 which gave a firm and specific guarantee of Northern Ireland's constitutional position. Section 1 (2) said:

> It is hereby declared that Northern Ireland remains part of His Majesty's dominions and of the United Kingdom and it is hereby affirmed that in no event will Northern Ireland or any part thereof cease to be part of His Majesty's dominions and of the United Kingdom without the consent of the Parliament of Northern Ireland

The foregoing might suggest that Northern Ireland was firmly wedded to the constitutional bedrock of the United Kingdom. That was not so. The Government of Ireland Act 1920 was merely the latest attempt to solve the Anglo-Irish problem in a situation of declining governmental control in Ireland. Its provisions were:

> ... dictated with a view to political pacification rather than administrative efficiency. When Southern Ireland broke away from British rule, the Act was amended in form so as to be rendered applicable to Northern Ireland alone. But it was not amended in subtance. As a consequence, powers were delegated to Northern Ireland which had been drafted to meet a quite different situation. *No regard was paid to the needs of the six counties as a political and economic unit.*[5]

There were other difficulties. The IRA had launched determined attacks on Northern Ireland, until the civil war forced them to desist. Members of the new government were conscious of the limiting financial provisions of the 1920 Act. And no one was yet sure of the precise boundaries of the new polity. So external threat and financial and political uncertainty provided a shallow foundation for the new constitution.

The Westminster model?
A parliamentary system of government modelled on Westminster was imposed on Northern Ireland in 1921. Parliament was bicameral. The upper house, the Senate, was composed of two ex-officio members, the Lord Mayor of Belfast and the Mayor of

Londonderry, and 24 members elected by the Commons by a system of proportional representation. The House of Commons consisted of 52 members elected by universal suffrage for a period of no more than five years. The method of election was the single transferable vote system, but by 1929 the Government reverted to the simple plurality system in accordance with Westminster practice. With minor exceptions parliamentary procedure followed the Westminster example.

The Crown's representative after the post of Lord Lieutenant was abolished in 1922, was the Governor. His duties included summarising, proroguing and dissolving Parliament, reading the Queen's Speech at the beginning of each session, resolving conflict between the two houses, and giving or withholding consent to legislation on the monarch's advice. His term of office was for six years and he could be reappointed. There were five governors altogether between 1921 and 1972 when the constitution was suspended.

The Governor appointed members of the Privy Council of Northern Ireland and Ministers to such government departments as the Parliament of Northern Ireland established. These departments were headed by Cabinet Ministers who had to be members of the Northern Ireland Parliament or became members within six months of appointment. In 1921 the Cabinet consisted of the Prime Minister's Department, and the Ministries of Finance, Home Affairs, Labour, Commerce, Agriculture and Education. By 1972 the Ministry of Labour had disappeared, but Departments of Development, Health and Social Services, and Community Relations had been added.

The powers exercised by the Government and Parliament of Northern Ireland became a matter of dispute. What we can say is that constitutionally it was a subordinate legislature. Section 75 of the 1920 Act stated:

> Notwithstanding the establishment of the Parliaments of Southern and Northern Ireland, or the Parliament of Ireland or anything contained in this Act, the supreme authority of the Parliament of the United Kingdom shall remain unaffected and undiminished over all persons, matters, and things in Ireland and every part thereof.

The local parliament was expected 'to make laws for the peace, order and good government of the area subject to certain specific exceptions, reservations and restrictions'. Parliament could only legislate on matters within its own territory, unlike the British dominions, which can regulate the actions of their citizens while abroad. It had no power to legislate on the 'excepted' matters. These included the Crown and succession, the making of peace or war, the armed forces, foreign affairs, external trade, coinage and legal tender. In addition a number of 'reserved' matters, which it had been originally intended to transfer to an all-Ireland parliament, were set aside. These included the postal service, the Supreme Court, certain reserved taxes including customs and excise, income tax, surtax, and any tax on profits or capital levy.

We can summarise the legislative powers transferred to Belfast thus:

> Put positively, the Northern Ireland Parliament may legislate on matters relating to law and order, to the police, to courts other than the Supreme Court, to civil and criminal law, to local government, to health and social services, to education, to planning and development, to commerce and industrial development and internal trade, to agriculture and to finance.[6]

That was the theory: much more enlightening is the practice. Westminster realised its onerous task in trying to find unity in diversity. It was mindful of the politics of a divided community and paid some obeisance to minority problems. Thus the system of election; it was hoped that proportional representation would help minorities to achieve parliamentary representation. Thus s. 5 of the Act which absolutely debarred the Northern Ireland Parliament from making laws interfering with religious equality or taking religious property without compensation. And thus the conciliatory words of King George V when he opened the Houses of Parliament in Belfast in 1921: 'I speak from a full heart when I pray that my coming to Ireland today may prove to be the first step towards the end of strife among her people, whatever their race or creed.' There was rioting in the streets while he spoke.

Of greater importance was the section concerning the Council of Ireland. 'With a view to the eventual establishment of a Parliament for the whole of Ireland', s. 2(1) of the Act created a Council of Ireland to encourage co-operation between the two Irelands. It was to have exclusive jurisdiction in the non-contentious matters of railways, fisheries and animal diseases, and could delegate further powers to itself if both parliaments agreed. Unionists chose their members but the Council never functioned. Craig had satisfied Collins, when they met at the Colonial Office in January 1922, that backwoodsmen on either side would introduce an air of acrimony into Council decisions and that nothing would be achieved. He suggested regular meetings at governmental level,[7] but, in the meantime, relations deteriorated so that even these collapsed.

Finally, Lloyd George's promise to the southern Irish that he would establish a Boundary Commission to 'determine in accordance with the wishes of the inhabitants, so far as may be compatible with economic and geographic conditions, the boundaries between Northern Ireland and the rest of Ireland' held out some hopes for the Catholic minority in Northern Ireland: Already 21 local councils, including that of the second city, had had to be dissolved for refusing to recognise the new authorities. The majority of these were in border areas. Unionists were not enthusiastic and refused to appoint one of the three commissioners. Eventually the British Government made the appointment. The report, completed in 1925, angered many nationalists who had expected to see large tracts of South Down, South Armagh, Fermanagh and Tyrone transferred to the Free State. So the Boundary Commission was a failure. It embittered the nationalist minority and created uncertainty among unionists while it deliberated.

While these palliatives were a recognition that there was communal division none of them offered a solution. Later examples of constitution-making – Tanganyika in 1951 and Fiji, in 1970,[8] for instance – show that Britain was capable of devising constitutions which, at least, attempted a solution to the communal problem.

The significance of institutions

Whatever be the historical reasons for the existence of the Stormont Government and Parliament, and whatever their merits and demerits in practice, it cannot be disputed that the system contributes powerfully to [this] misrepresentation: the whole vocabulary of three governments, Westminster, Belfast and Dublin, implants the notion that there are somehow three coordinate states, and that, as two of them are geographically on the same island, Westminster is the 'third man out'.[9]

The misrepresentation of institutions has been commented upon by another British ally of Unionism. T. E. Utley believed that Britain classified Ireland as something more akin to a colonial than a domestic problem: 'Paradoxically, it was proclaimed in the almost ludicrously impressive array of institutions with which the Province of Northern Ireland was equipped at the very outset of its existence'.[10]

It was for that reason that Ulster Unionists turned from reluctant devolutionists into anti-integrationists within a decade. A subordinate legislature cut off from Westminster by the physical and psychological barrier of the Irish Sea, infiltrated and surrounded by 'rebels to the Crown' could not flourish. Sir James Craig sought to overcome this lack of confidence: 'There must be a dignity about our Parliament and that Parliament must be very deeply rooted in Ulster's soil, so that no opponent dare come forward at any time and say of that great structure . . . "that it is only a small affair and we can easily sweep it to one side".'[11]

The Parliament building was not completed until 1932 and was situated on an imposing site at Stormont, a Belfast suburb; thoughtfully outside the riot-torn city of Belfast and on a hill, it is one of the few Parliament buildings in the world deliberately removed from the main city centre. At that time, 27 per cent of the governing party were in receipt of official salaries. (The comparable figure for Westminster was about 8 per cent.) Charges of government extravagance grew. Following Unionist election losses in 1925, a loyalist newspaper complained: 'That the Government has suffered because of extravagance is not open to doubt. The initial mistake was made four years ago of imitating the Imperial Parliament and creating huge but quite unnecessary Departments . . .'[12]

The strictures were ignored. Sir James Craig (created Lord Craigavon in 1927) made extravagance an art of government. He pursued a policy of 'distributing bones' even at times of financial stringency throughout the United Kingdom. There were political advantages to be gained by talking to people on the ground. He was prepared to go to inordinate lengths to discuss the most trivial topics with local councillors and regularly undertook provincewide tours at an estimated cost of £100,000 each. His achievements were considerable. From inauspicious beginnings he had moulded the parliamentary institutions into an ideological weapon and had produced the 'conditional loyalist': 'The Sinn Fein Unionist who was thus produced ... came to regard himself as a part of Britain only insofar as Britain was capable of maintaining, on his behalf, the frontiers of his territory . . .'[13] This attitude reached its apogee in the 1936 Ulster Unionist Council Reports. 'Northern Ireland without a Parliament of her own would be a standing temptation to certain British politicians to make another bid for a final settlement with the Irish Republic.'

It is instructive to examine the extent to which the Stormont system mirrored the Westminster model. The administration of the province was in the hands of the Northern Ireland Civil Service, which (after 1925) was open to anyone who passed a competitive examination. Its creation highlighted the difficulties of establishing an impartial administration. Most civil servants were recruited from the old Irish administration in Dublin. Some came from Whitehall, notably from Sir James Craig's old department, the Admiralty. It was calculated that 5 per cent of the staff were British, a figure that was much higher in the most senior grades. Although some Catholics were appointed to very senior posts their numbers dropped consistently throughout the late 1920s and early 1930s: 'As the years passed clear evidence increased of Orange Order surveillance of Catholic civil servants and even of civil servants married to Catholics. Prominent and respectable Unionists like Sir Robert Lynn (editor of the *Northern Whig*) and Sir Charles Blackmore (Cabinet Secretary) acted as 'go-betweens' between the Order and the government in these matters.'[14] So the Civil Service serves as a reminder of the fact that, as with so many things in Northern Ireland, we have to distinguish between the quality of its work and its political composition.

The role of Governor can be little faulted. All the incumbents faithfully carried out their duties as representatives of a constitutional monarch. A Governor exercised his veto powers on Stormont legislation on only one occasion – the Local Government Bill 1922 – and that was at the behest of his Westminster masters. The Senate may have been modelled on the House of Lords but was unlike it in two respects: its original function was envisaged as the protection of minorities, and its members were elected. It never fulfilled that function because it was a pale reflection of the Commons which elected it. Nor did it measure up to the majesty of the Lords.

Stormont followed the Westminster model if we accept that the party with a parliamentary majority has unfettered power. But that model presupposes an alternating two-party system of government which has never operated in Northern Ireland. In that respect Northern Ireland was more akin to the Continental political system: 'Calculating a majority by excluding a major party is alien to English politics. It is however a familiar and necessary procedure in societies such as France and Italy, where those who govern must face the fact that they do so without the allegiance of all parties in the state.'[15] It followed Continental practices, too, in using proportional representation for its first two general elections.

Unionists probably believed themselves to be pursuing the Whitehall version of the Westminster model. Emphasis was placed on the right of the executive to make decisions – inevitable perhaps considering that Stormont was a half-time affair, sitting on three half-days per week and enjoying long recesses (it met for 43 days in 1933 and 25 in 1941). A strident law and order programme was to the fore. Generally the 'Unionist party's bland assurance that its "natural majority" gave it a right to rule in perpetuity; its aggressive attachment to linguistic symbols, songs, and speeches, its entrenched resistance to any attempt to attenuate the powers of its own executive – all of this, including its enthusiastic if ambiguous loyalty to the Crown, is intelligible within the conservative version of the British model'.[16]

With the collapse of Stormont and the introduction of direct rule in 1972 it has become fashionable to view the Northern Ireland government and administration as corrupt and inept. The truth is more complex. The fact is that 'the structure was from the beginning inherently flawed, and that those who pulled the levers of the governmental machine have not been wholly to blame for the downhill path that has been followed'.[17] Briefly, we can say that the 1920 Act established a subordinate legislature in Belfast, but its institutions came to play a role out of all proportions to their original intention and consequently there developed 'Sinn Fein Unionism', a form of nascent Ulster nationalism.

Law and order

In assessing the institutions and practices of government in Northern Ireland it is never possible to move very far from the tumultuous origins of the State.[18] Between 1920 and 1922 nearly 300 people were killed, most of them in Belfast, in what was virtually a civil war. In 1922 alone 232 people were killed (including two Unionist MPs), nearly 1,000 were wounded, 400 were interned, and more than £3 million worth of property was destroyed. A curfew existed in Belfast until 1924.

The draftsmen of the 1920 Act knew that security would be a major feature in the inception of the new parliament. One reason for Britain's withdrawal was war weariness, a belief that she had tried too long to hold the peace in Ireland. The Northern Ireland Government were expected to secure 'peace, order and good government', yet in the first few months the new Government had control neither over the Armed Services (an 'excepted' matter) nor the Royal Irish Constabulary (a 'reserved' matter). As a result of the continuing warfare that was soon rectified, and by 1922 Northern Ireland had a ratio of one policeman to every six families. We shall see that the police have been uniquely important and contentious in Northern Ireland.

The Royal Ulster Constabulary. The main law enforcement service was the RUC, established by the Constabulary Act (NI) on 1 June 1922 in succession to the Royal Irish Constabulary founded in 1836. It was like its predecessor in two respects: executive control was highly centralised; and it was generally seen as a military rather than a police force. The Hunt Report noted:

> The most striking difference between the RUC and the police forces elsewhere in the United Kingdom is that it fulfils a military as well as a civilian role . . . in Northern Ireland the military role has understandably been regarded as of first importance and has played a significant part via the training, equipment and traditions of the force. The impression of a military force is strengthened by the close association of the force with the Ulster Special Constabulary which, at least in the rural areas of the Province, is almost wholly devoted to security duties of a military kind.[19]

Control of the force was invested in the Inspector General, who was answerable to the Minister of Home Affairs. No attempt was made to appoint local watch committees to make it appear independent of the Government. One third of all RUC places was to be set aside for Catholic recruits, but by 1969 only eleven per cent of the RUC were

Catholics, a figure which was fairly typical of Catholic membership at any time. In the early days any Catholic who might be tempted to join faced IRA intimidation and communal ostracism. Catholics looked on the police as a Protestant force. They had justification for this attitude since, in the 1920s when R. Dawson Bates, the first Minister of Home Affairs, had founded an RUC Orange Lodge in January 1923 and, without any trace of irony, called it the Robert Peel Lodge. Its first Worshipful Master, District Inspector J. W. Nixon, was dismissed from the force in 1924 for making a political speech. He had warned Orangemen of an imminent *airborne* invasion by the Free State army! During these years there were many complaints about promotion, the substance of which was that Englishmen were getting jobs which should be going to Orangemen.[20]

The 'B' Specials. As Hunt has noted, the RUC must be studied alongside the Ulster Special Constabulary (more popularly known as the 'B' Specials). They owed their existence to the Special Constables Act (1914) which gave the Crown powers to enrol Special Constables when war-time conditions dictated. Many of the original recruits were members of the illegal UVF which had been reformed under Colonel Wilfrid Spender. By 1920 the UVF was still an unofficial force with no power to carry arms. Spender and Sir Basil Brooke, a large landowner and future Prime Minister, sought official recognition for the force. By an Order in Council in 1920, recruiting began for a Special Constabulary in Ulster.

Three classes were formed: Class A, full-time men enlisted in the RIC for a period of six months, Class B, part-time recruits, Class C, a reserve organised along semi-military lines consisting of men available only in an emergency. Classes A and C were eventually disbanded, but the 'B' Specials were made a permanent force under the command of the Inspector General of Police and the Minister of Home Affairs. They held much the same power, privileges and authority as the RUC and were organised along similar lines. By the middle of 1922 there were 50,000 full- and part-time policemen in Northern Ireland, supported by 13 battalions of British troops financed by the British government but controlled by the Northern Ireland government. The question of responsibility for the maintenance of the 'B' Specials embarrassed Westminster. In 1922 the Chancellor of the Exchequer 'proposed to make available £1,475,000 for payment of the special constabulary but he proposed to do this in the estimates in a vote making provision for unemployment and other service in Ulster "so as to avoid if possible raising a controversy in Parliament in regard to this force'''.[21] The Government's intention was that the force would relieve the troops in Ireland.

On 1 August 1969 the strength of the 'B' Specials was 425 full-time and 8,481 part-time constables, *none* of whom were Catholics. Opponents of the Government maintained that from the beginning the 'B' Specials were the Orange Order in uniform, part of the armed wing of the executive, poorly trained and ill disciplined.

The Special Powers Act

> To meet the difficulties occasioned by a virtual state of civil war and invasion in 1922 the Parliament of Northern Ireland enacted the Civil Authorities [Special Powers] Act . . . The result of the Act, when taken in conjunction with the existence of the Special Constabulary [then 44,000 men] was that apart from the establishment of military courts, the Government enjoyed powers similar to those current in time of martial law.[22]

The essential point of the Act was that it transferred many peace preservation powers from the judiciary to the executive. Power rested with the Minister of Home Affairs (or any Parliamentary Secretary or officer of the RUC to whom he might delegate his powers) who could 'take all such steps and issue all such orders as may be necessary for preserving the peace and order' (s. 1). Similarly s. 2 (4) contains a comprehensive provision: 'If any person does any act of such a nature as to be calculated to be prejudicial to the preservation of the peace or maintenance of order in Northern Ireland and not specifically provided for in the regulations, he shall be deemed to be guilty of an offence against the regulations.' Sweeping power indeed! Provision was made for advisory panels to assist the Minister but they were discarded.

The Act was renewed annually from 1922 to 1933 and then made permanent (until 1972). Given conditions in 1922, the existence of such a statute might be acceptable, but its permanency suggests that either Northern Ireland was ungovernable or that the executive did not operate the liberal democratic model. The events of the past few years might suggest the former; and yet '. . . between the early 1920s and late 1960s Ireland enjoyed a longer period of freedom from major internal disturbance than it had known since the first half of the eighteenth century'.[23]

Security became a way of life. The Government and Parliament were born in violence. Paramilitary law enforcers were trained by, and closely identified with, the State; draconian measures were introduced, and after a few years violence subsided. What was the Government to do? In the end they fell back on the 'security response', repressing violence by whatever means they considered necessary, regardless of legal constraints. For almost fifty years this proved effective, but at a cost. Citizens became accustomed to the belief that the rule of law must always be suspended. It failed to bring the disaffected minority in from the cold. But all this did not amount to 'a police state':

> It does not ... conform to the traditional model of a police state such as that of Fouché in post-revolutionary France, for neither the RUC or the USC can be classified as a protector, moral guide or censor to the community, albeit that in one sense they constitute a form of state apparat. However much they reflect the policies and values of the Northern Ireland Government, neither the RUC nor the USC dominated the style of government or internal policy as did the Police in the Weimar Republic. Nor in any sense can Northern Ireland be classified as a totalitarian police state, for the Police have not gained supremacy over the Army, Judiciary or Administrative and Civil Services in Northern Ireland. ...[24]

Civil liberties

> A basic paradox of democratic government is that political decisions presuppose rule by the majority, whereas judicial decisions presuppose the rule of law. In a representative assembly, the majority wins; the minority always loses. In the courts, by contrast, judges do not count heads but weigh arguments.[25]

The 1920 Act specifically guarantees only one civil liberty – freedom of religion – and that was challenged only once in the courts (in 1929). In fact, technically there were eight liberties denied by the (amended) Special Powers Act 1954. They included freedom of speech and press, of assembly, of association, trial by jury and freedom from arrest without warrant. In other respects Northern Ireland does not differ overmuch from the English tradition since 'British standards make no provision for protecting minority rights, because the British Constitution does not provide for justiciable rights'.[26]

This has not been a major concern in Britain, where the Government has enjoyed legitimacy. In Northern Ireland, however, recourse to the courts may have had an ameliorative effect. We can illustrate this point by making a comparison between the nature of civil rights agitation in the United States and in Northern Ireland. The American Negro readily used the courts to redress any alleged grievances – he knew his rights under the written constitution. In contrast, Ulster Catholics used the courts infrequently because the absence of any formal guarantees in the British constitution of basic rights meant that there was no tradition of civil rights litigation. Black Americans have demonstrated in support of judicial decisions rather than in defiance of the law. Ulster Catholics have not had that confidence, particularly since the English tradition 'emphasises the defencelessness of an electoral minority under the Stormont system in the absence of legally scheduled rights enforceable through the courts against the powers that be'.[27] Basically Catholics believed that the courts were 'loaded' against them because the majority of judicial appointments have been made from the ranks of Unionism.

Financial provisions

> The history of Northern Ireland's financial relations with Great Britain has been one of evading the consequences of the Government of Ireland Act 1920.[28]

The 1920 Act envisaged that Northern Ireland would have sufficient revenue to finance the transferred services and make a payment known as the 'Imperial Contribution' i.e. services such as the armed forces, defence, the national debt, and other items falling on the British exchequer. It was denied the power to raise whatever revenues were necessary for the proper government of the area. Stormont was to be given a comfortable income and left to its own devices.

Ulster politicians realised that it could not work. By mid-September 1921 Sir James Craig was appealing to London for £130,000 to keep the Northern administration afloat. He realised that the Dublin authorities hoped that these financial impositions would drive Ulster in their direction. All this was played out against a background of exceptionally high unemployment.

To understand how financial relations were expected to work we shall rely on Martin Wallace's detailed description:

> Even at the beginning, some eighty-eight per cent of Northern Ireland's revenue was levied by the British Government, and 'transferred revenue' raised by local taxes has always been a small proportion of the total. Reserved taxes include customs and excise duties, income tax and supertax, and various profits taxes. From these are deducted the cost of operating reserved services in Northern Ireland; these include the inland revenue and customs and excise departments, the Supreme Court, the Post Office and the British Broadcasting Corporation. A further deduction, known as the imperial contribution, is made ... The 'residuary share of reserved revenue' is then transferred to the Northern Ireland exchequer. Taxes transferred to the Northern Ireland Parliament include death duties, stamp duties, entertainments duty and motor vehicle duty. Responsibility for the allocation of the reserved revenue rests with a statutory Joint Exchequer Board, consisting of representatives of the Treasury and the Ministry of Finance, with a chairman appointed by the Crown; in practice this is likely to mean approving a division of revenue already agreed by Stormont and Whitehall, and there have been long periods when the board has not met. The board ... can arbitrate in other issues arising from the financial relations between the two governments.[29]

Controversy first arose over the fixed contribution to the 'Imperial Contribution'. It was estimated that Northern Ireland would have to pay £7.92 million but this proved to be over-optimistic. A special arbitration committee to fix a more realistic figure was chaired by Lord Colwyn. It decided in 1925 that the 'Imperial Contribution' was no longer to be a first charge on Northern Ireland's revenue. Instead, the Government's own expenditure was to be the first charge, increasing in line with expenditure in Britain. The 'Imperial Contribution' became anything that was left in Northern Ireland's budget. Consequently the contribution varied from year to year – as little as £10,000 in the 1930s and as much as £36.3 million in 1944–45. It has served as a barometer of Northern Ireland's prosperity.

The Colwyn Committee had gone a long way towards undermining a major principle of the 1920 Act by envisaging that the

'Imperial Contribution' might be reduced to vanishing point. At a practical level 'it provided a strong disincentive to the exercise of Northern Ireland's power to vary its own taxes'.[30] There were some departures from the principle of parity in taxation. The complexity of the financial relationship grew with Ulster's increasing social and economic difficulties. The Unemployment Insurance Agreement (1926) provided if in any year 'the payment by the Northern Ireland Exchequer to its Unemployment Fund exceeded, per head of population, the corresponding payment by the United Kingdom Government to the Great Britain Fund, then the United Kingdom Exchequer would meet three-quarters of the excess'. Other agreements transferred United Kingdom funds to Northern Ireland for specific purposes, thereby supplementing the revenue from taxation due under the 1920 Act.

In 1938 the principle of parity was accepted; under this the United Kingdom ensured that Ulster could have the same social services and the same standards as the mainland if the Northern Ireland budget deficit was not the result of local extravagance. However, that did not go far enough in alleviating the dreadful social conditions which Northern Ireland had inherited in 1921, and in 1944 it was accepted that Ulster needed special expenditure to make up a substantial leeway on services such as housing, schools and hospitals. The growth of the welfare state added to her difficulties. An interim agreement (1946) provided for special transfers of mainland funds to meet expenditure on unemployment insurance, unemployment assistance and family allowance. Finally, the Social Services Agreement (1948) granted Northern Ireland special payments to meet national insurance and other social benefits.

These agreements had a number of curious results. Firstly the financial relationship was little understood by the general public. Both Governments continued to pay obeisance to the financial provisions of the 1920 Act, so that the annual presentation of a separate budget at Stormont conjured up in the minds of the public a picture of an independent country deciding its own revenue and paying its way as a member of the United Kingdom. The reality was somewhat different. Not until budget day in London could Stormont work out its own revenue for taxation. An ex-Comptroller and Auditor General for Northern Ireland has described the result: '... The "King's Speech" in Northern Ireland ... frequently makes no mention of pending highly important and controversial legislation, because the party in power in Great Britain has not yet shown its hand. The speech becomes an anaemic document, full of platitudes for the past and pieties for the future'.[31]

Secondly it created tension between Unionists. It was not easy to accept that Ulster might be subsidised by Westminster. Thus the Minister of Finance explained, 'The misconception has arisen in some quarters that this payment (Northern Ireland's share of Reversed Taxes) is a form of subsidy, whereas it almost entirely represents a net payment out of the gross proceeds of United Kingdom taxation imposed on Northern Ireland.'[32] When times were good the illusion of the sovereign legislature could be maintained, but when times were bad Westminster could be used as a ready scapegoat. In March 1961, for instance, with growing unemployment in the Belfast area a Unionist backbencher warned: 'The Government must make up its mind whether it owes loyalty to the Conservative Party or to the working people of Belfast.' Financial dependence made regional self-government something of a fiction. When direct rule was imposed in 1972 and Northern Ireland received less favourable attention from the Treasury some influential voices raised the possibility of a Unilateral Declaration of Independence. There can be little doubt that the myths surrounding the financial provision of the 1920 Act encouraged this idea.

Conclusion

The 1920 Act was imposed upon Ireland and accepted reluctantly in Ulster. Faced with the conflicting demands of Irishmen, with little sympathy and less understanding of Ireland, the coalition cabinet bowed at the altar of expediency. It produced a constitution that was virtually still-born; it was, according to F. H. Newark, a 'legislative ruin' within seven months of its passing. It broke one of the cardinal rules enunciated by Carl Friedrich: 'The constitution . . . is the process by which governmental action is effectively restrained,'[33] – and yet it endured. Its durability was a monument to Unionist tenacity and British empiricism. But while its supporters basked in its majesty, its opponents undermined its foundations.

3 A Divided Society

Ulster (indeed) provides an illustration of the fact that a real understanding of a socially divided society, however its groups be defined, depends not only on an analysis of the political and economic structure at the top but also on an examination of the society at the grass-roots level.

Rosemary Harris[1]

We came very early to our politics. One learned, quite literally at one's mother's knee, that Christ died for the human race and Patrick Pearse for the Irish section of it.

Eamonn McCann[2]

. . . a display of political slogans on a Belfast house, 'No Pope here. No surrender. God save the Queen.' The three standard slogans of Protestant Ulster.

Richard Rose[3]

Demography

Opponents of the Northern Ireland regime refer to it contemptuously as a 'statelet' or 'the Six Counties' to compare its diminutive size and powers with its pretentious claims to sovereignty. It is indeed a small territory, with a population of one and a half million, less than 3 per cent that of the United Kingdom, a land mass smaller than that of Yorkshire, and a rateable value (1970) of £14 million, whereas, to take one example, that of the City of Leeds was £22 million.

It was primarily an agricultural region, with about 90 per cent of the total area devoted to agriculture, and just over 50 per cent of its population living on the land. The political and economic geography of the province is important. The course of the River Bann divides east from west. Counties Antrim and Down and the City of Belfast lie in the prosperous, industrialised east. County Armagh is a sort of halfway house, and counties Londonderry, Tyrone and Fermanagh lie in the relatively underdeveloped west. In the beginning two groups of industries – textiles (mainly linen) and shipbuilding (and allied industries) – were the staples, absorbing about 50 per cent of the labour force. They were concentrated in the Greater Belfast area, where 63 per cent of the population lived by 1937. This uneven balance of industry encouraged a net shift of population from the west to the east and led to charges of regional discrimination: 'Time and again it was made clear to me that Belfast Unionist politicians were suspected of being potentially ready to sacrifice the welfare of areas distant from the capital, and especially those on the border ...'.[4] Richard Rose's Loyalty Survey verified that opinion by illustrating that dissatisfaction with the regime was stronger among Protestants in the west than in the east.

A major complaint concerned the location of industry. Belfast, as the seat of the Industrial Revolution, had been used to persuade Protestant workers that their economic interests lay within the United Kingdom. After 1921, Belfast totally dominated the province when partition downgraded the second city. Derry ceased trading with Donegal and Sligo in the Irish Free State and was thrown into uneven competition with Belfast. By the mid 1930s 61 per cent of all jobs in the manufacturing industries were in Belfast County Borough. By 1944 the Government accepted the need to site new industries in provincial towns, but this policy was not wholly successful. Of 217 new firms established with government assistance between 1945–66, only 9 per cent went west of the Bann. Even the creation of a new city, begun in 1966, to relieve congestion in Belfast was only 48 kilometres from the capital. And finally virtually all imports flowed through the ports of Belfast and Larne 34 kilometres away. They handled £743 million worth in 1972, leaving the remaining £54 million worth to the other ports in the province.

The East–West divide also mirrored the religious cleavage in the province – 71 per cent of the population in the east were Protestant, and three-fifths of the population in the peripheral areas were Catholic. That seemed to suggest that Stormont was more interested in looking after 'loyal' Protestants. The truth was not quite as simple as that, but that was still the way in which poor Catholics perceived their plight.

A closer examination of the statistics suggests that there was some validity in this perception. The first census (1926) revealed that 33.5 per cent of the population were Catholic, 31.3 per cent Presbyterian,

27 per cent Church of Ireland, 3.9 per cent Methodist, and 4.3 per cent others. These figures remained fairly stable until recent years: the (estimated) Catholic population had risen to 36.8 per cent by 1971. Given its higher birth rate – 45.5 per cent of children under one year of age in 1971 were Catholic – one might have expected a substantial increase in the Catholic population. In fact the surplus has been removed by emigration and changing attitudes to birth control. Baritt and Carter estimate that between 1937–61 a clear majority of emigrants were Catholics.[5] More recent evidence suggests that this trend was reversed in the following decade, and that the rate of emigration from some of the younger Protestant age groups actually increased. Furthermore, data collected by the Ulster Pregnancy Advisory Association (UPAA), a pressure group to assist women to obtain legal abortions, indicate 'the rapidity with which Roman Catholic attitudes to family planning are changing'. Since 1970 the number of Catholics using the UPAA has risen consistently.

The bare statistics mask a subculture of distrust and must be analysed against a socio-economic background of high unemployment and a low standard of living. In fact socio-economic problems pervade the whole history of Northern Ireland and will be examined in greater detail later. For the moment we need only note the perceptions each side held. 'The Government has deliberately committed all of its resources East of the Bann to force us out of the province,' complains the underprivileged Catholic living in the west. 'Catholics are trying to outbreed us,' warn vigilant Protestants, 'so that they can drive us into a united Ireland.' Both 'truths' can be challenged but this will make little impact on the activists, who have the certitude of group solidarity and the means to protect their own territory.

Religion

> We are brought back, inescapably, to what so many people seek to deny: the rather obvious fact of a conflict between groups defined by *religion*. This does not mean it is a theological war.[6]

Northern Ireland has the highest degree of religiosity (a measure of how important people think religion is and of how far they endorse traditional beliefs) in the United Kingdom. An Independent Television Authority (ITA) survey (1970) noted that 22 per cent in the

United Kingdom and 57 per cent in Northern Ireland were in the highest religiosity groups, and 25 per cent and 5 per cent respectively were in the lowest groups. Arend Lijphart has examined the correlation between religion and political affiliation in Northern Ireland, the United States, Britain, Australia, Canada, West Germany, the Netherlands and Switzerland, and concluded that the 'index of religious voting' for Northern Ireland was of an unprecedented magnitude.[7] We can confidently say, then, that religion is of considerably greater importance in Northern Ireland than in the United Kingdom generally, and that one's religious views influence one's political judgement.

It does not necessarily follow that the conflict is at heart a 'holy war'. Forty-three per cent of Richard Rose's respondents defined their nationality as 'Irish', 29 per cent as 'British', and 21 per cent as 'Ulster'. The nationality problem is important, but, for the moment, it is more useful to recognise that religious differences coincide with different political allegiances. The conflict, then, is between Ulster Protestants and Irish Catholics.

The Protestants

> I may be a bad Christian but I'm a good Protestant.[8]
> We want to stay British, whether you bloody English like it or not.[9]

We have already noted that a recurring theme in Ulster's history has been inter-denominational conflict among Protestants, especially Episcopalians and Presbyterians. The social anthropoligist Rosemary Harris discovered that this conflict carried over into contemporary life and was, in fact, much stronger than in modern England. It spilled over into the political arena with damaging consequences for the Unionist party.

Two pieces of legislation in 1923 illustrate that the Unionist monolith was not as secure as is sometimes supposed, and that the party had to concern itself with moral and social issues as well as the border question. The first concerns the Licensing Act (NI) which established the opening hours of public houses and was considered too liberal by the temperance movement. In effect they were prohibitionists who received clerical – particularly Presbyterian – support. They failed to amend the Act, although they did challenge the Government in the 1929 General Election when three of their

(Local Option) candidates contested Unionist seats. None of them succeeded; but they did demonstrate that the Unionist party would have to move with some stealth if it were not to be undermined from within.

The second example, the Education Act, and subsequent education legislation, had a more divisive effect. No less than three Ministers of Education – Lords Londonderry and Charlemont, and Samuel Hall-Thompson – resigned their posts prematurely, surely making that Department the most casualty-prone at Stormont. Opponents of the 1923 Act detected secular tendencies in it, even though the (Anglican) Archbishop of Armagh considered that it secured for Protestants 'practically all that we desire'. The United Education Committee of the Protestant Churches, probably the most effective Unionist promotional pressure group in the history of the province, held a mass meeting in March 1925, chaired by the Moderator of the Presbyterian Church in Ireland, and attended by, among others, representatives of the Belfast County Grand Orange Lodge, to demand amendments to the legislation. The gathering was too representative to be ignored, and the timing was impeccable – the Prime Minister was about to open the 1925 election campaign. The 1923 Act was amended later that year.

That victory set the trend. An American historian, who has chronicled the education debate, summarised the position:

> ... the Protestant clerics triumphed not only over their religious rivals, but over the state as well, a fact which leads one to observe that, ironically, the partition of Ireland did not change the basic state-Church conflict in education, but only the groups involved in the fray ... the Protestant clergy in the north have followed the same strategy of maximising their own powers that always has been followed by the Roman Catholic clergy in the south.[10]

We must not allow these controversies to obscure the degree of Protestant unity – after all, its raison d'être was maintenance of the border and resistance to 'Rome rule'. Presbyterians and Methodists, for example, had established official inter-church relations as early as 1904. The major Protestant confessions had united in 1911 to oppose the Papal Decree *Ne Temere*. The body which became The Irish Council of Churches, incorporating the major Protestant denominations, first met in 1923. (The ecumenical spirit was slow to include

Catholicism: by 1956 the only contact between the Catholic and Reformed Churches was their common membership of the Churches Industrial Council). So the public disagreements among the Churches were more significant at the political level because they demonstrated the fragility of the Unionist monolith on certain issues.

It is in this context that we must examine the political leanings of Protestant fundamentalism: 'Ulster is the last bastion of Bible Protestantism in Europe,' warns the Rev. Ian Paisley, 'and as such she stands the sole obstacle at this time against the great objective of the Roman See – a unified Roman Catholic Europe.' In an era of declining church attendance the phenomenal rise of his Free Presbyterian Church, emphatically not a part of the official Presbyterian Church, is witness to a durable tradition in Ulster Protestantism. From a modest beginning in 1951 he now possesses more than 40 churches in the North of Ireland, is on the 'evangelical circuit' of Australia, North America and Hong Kong, and has his headquarters in what is reputedly the largest Protestant church building constructed in Europe since 1945. All of this must be particularly galling to mainstream Protestantism struggling to maintain its membership.

Abrasive anti-Catholicism and anti-ecumenism largely explain its success. Paisley, its founder and Moderator, is a politician and preacher of considerable political skill and great demagogic powers. But it would be a mistake to imagine that fundamentalism is simply the personification of Paisley: his departure would not mean the end of 'Paisleyism' since it represents one of 'two common Protestant types: the confident and the fearful'. 'Catholics don't really exist for the confident', whereas the 'fearful' is 'hyperconscious of the Catholic presence'.[11]

Both types see Catholicism as a monolith, but it is the 'fearful' which explains the high level of religious practice and the correlation between religion and political affiliation in Northern Ireland. A sociologist makes the seductively simple point which sees:

> . . . religion as defence, comfort and re-assurance against dark and sinister forces which threaten human existence . . . it is necessary to have a demonstrable religious affiliation in Northern Ireland because this is the means to have roots, friends, group membership and a social identity – all the characteristics necessary for social

survival. This is how you know who you are and, equally important, who you are not. Religion is the servant of the social need for location in a divided and threatened society: church membership is the institutional expression of that need.[12]

And it is the existence of the 'fearful' which explains the continuing phenomenon of the Orange Order. Orangeism is 'organised Protestantism' designed to overcome interdenominational conflict and the social tensions prevalent among Protestants. A geographer's examination of two interlocking areas in Belfast, one Catholic–Protestant, and the other upper-class Protestant–working-class Protestant, arrived at the following conclusion: 'The lack of contact across the socio-economic divide of the Upper Malone Road would appear to be almost as great as the lack of contact across the religious divide in west Belfast'.[13]

The order probably played a 'healing' role within the Protestant camp. It helped to bridge the gap between adult and adolescent, admittedly by passing on prejudices from one generation to the next. (Ulster must be one of the very few Western societies which avoided the generational conflict of the late 1960s.) Its parades gave the individual an emotional attachment to his lodge and a sense of local pride vis-à-vis other Protestants. It may have been more successful than the Churches in bringing communities together; for example, only 20 per cent of Belfast's Sandy Row belonged to church groups but 33 per cent were members of the Orange Order. Its most important role was to serve as a social emollient as well as a stimulus to patriotic emotions:

Part of the anxiety to get local key men into the Lodge arose not only because it placed them in a situation in which their inherent superiority was denied, but because the man in the street could tell them publicly what he thought and yet not lose his reputation for 'modesty' . . . If loyal Protestantism were the real ultimate value, then the ordinary man knew that ultimately he was a more worthwhile person than 'the doctors and people of that sort' who 'don't make much difference in their religion'.[14]

Orangemen believe that the Order is a religious body united in its determination to uphold the principles of the Reformed confession. While there is validity in that point of view, it does not go nearly far enough because what strikes the outsider is its negative quality. It is much more than a quaint folklore society and its parades represent more than colourful expressions of that tradition. The latter, in fact, is 'a highly significant element in the sub-tribalism which is the kernel of the society. Its purpose is not only to display the trophies of each side's sucesses but also to delimit the territory each claims'.[15] Its anti-Catholicism is legendary and need not detain us. Its support in Belfast originally arose because it provided the usual friendly society benefits and it exercised strong nepotistic control. There is little reason to believe that nepotism has ceased to exist and none to imagine that anti-Catholicism has stopped.

A final unifying factor among Protestants is a sense of anti-Englishness. Patrick Buckland explains resentment of English politicians as one reason for the cohesion of Unionism.[16] Lord Brookeborough, a former Prime Minister, shared that view: 'Since I've become an Ulsterman I hate the English rather more.' And Rosemary Harris summarises the collective opinion: 'Their stereotype of the Englishman reflected in almost every detail the Englishman's wartime stereotype of the Prussian ... efficient but ruthless, subservient to rules and regulations to a comical extent, pompous, humourless, and often cruel. An additional English characteristic was to be a godless heathen. ...'[17] Protestantism and Unionism, then, are not interchangeable terms. Protestants are divided on social and denominational lines, although many are united in their anti-Catholicism and anti-Englishness. It has been the role of the Orange Order to bring them together in a religio-political institution to serve the interests of Unionism. Their lack of security, expressed in a siege mentality led them into an arid negativism:

> ... the primary group identity of these people is as 'the Protestant people of Northern Ireland' and they retain a strong sense of representing a long and nobly defended tradition of religious and political freedom, even if their main responses are of resistance to what threatens the freedoms rather than a positive cultivation of the tradition.[18]

The Catholics

The Protestant Church in Ireland – and the same is true of the Protestant Church anywhere else – is not only not the rightful representative of the early Irish Church, but is not even a part of the Church of Christ.[19]

Paradoxically, the Catholic minority have been more communally confident than the Protestants. They were all attached to the one Church which they attended in massive numbers: Rose reports a weekly attendance of 95 per cent in comparison to a Protestant 46 per cent attendance. Few Catholics felt the need to join a defensive sectarian organisation; the Ancient Order of Hibernians (AOH) attracted only 3 per cent of Catholics (the Orange Order had 19 per cent of Protestants). In fact 69 per cent of Catholics did not know what it stood for: typical resolutions at its annual parades pledged support for the Irish language, loyalty to the Pope, allegiance to the principle of a united Ireland, and anti-communism. It adopted its title in 1838 and attained its most popular appeal between 1905–14. Given the state of civic unrest, it suspended its annual demonstrations in 1969 and resumed them in 1975. It is unlikely that many people noticed either their disappearance or their resumption.[20] It was the Church which provided Catholics with their source of strength and loyalty.

Catholicism has to be seen in an all-Ireland context, comprising as it does 75 per cent of the population of the island. Its self-image was of the Church of the Penal Laws, the Church which had withstood persecution and given spiritual and political guidance to its flock; and after 1921, an exiled community separated from its co-religionists by an artificial and arbitrary boundary. From the beginning it refused to recognise the institutions of the state by ignoring all official invitations and failing to appoint a chaplain to Stormont. It has never contemplated assimilation but has turned its attention to Dublin.

In the Republic, Unionists noted, a steady decline in the Protestant population from just over 10 per cent in 1911 to approximately five per cent in 1961. They saw the Catholic social code being written into De Valera's 1937 Constitution, and two years later heard him proclaim in America, 'We are a Catholic nation.' They heard Ulster's Catholic Bishops pronounce with amazing insensitive insularity on the question of conscription:

Our people have already been subjected to the gravest injustice in being cut off from one of the oldest nations in Europe and in being deprived of their fundamental rights in their own land. In such circumstances to compel them to fight for their oppressor would be likely to raise them to indignation and resistance. (Statement read at masses on Sunday, 30 April 1939.)

Nonetheless, the opponents of Catholicism have exaggerated the depth of clerical dominance. Certainly Ireland is exceptional among Catholic nations in never having produced an anti-clerical party: 'The reason is not that Irish Catholics are uniformly docile, but that they are able to compartmentalise their loyalties, and to accept the Church's authority unquestioningly in one sphere at the very time that they challenge it in another.'[21] During parts of the nineteenth century the laity differed from the hierarchy on the land and home rule issues; in the past few decades, particularly since Vatican II (1962–65), many laymen have been highly critical of a conservative Church leadership on moral and social issues such as contraception and integrated education. On a wider plane, the accession of Pope John XXIII (1958–63) and the opening of the Second Vatican Council began an era of cordiality between the Christian denominations. Ecumenism became fashionable. In Austria, for example, the Archbishop of Vienna spoke of the need of the Church to perform an 'integrating function' in the modern democratic state in May 1963; no longer could the Church rule, he said, it could only serve. In the Netherlands, which had also seen a bitter Church-state conflict, a progressive Dutch hierarchy replaced a defensive Catholicism which had caused misunderstanding in the past. In Ireland some reconciliation was evident, but all the major Churches moved very cautiously.

On one issue Catholics appeared united. In Richard Rose's survey 73 per cent of Catholic respondents agreed with the statement that Catholics had been treated unfairly. They believed that they suffered discrimination of a psychological, political and economic nature. The question will be examined more closely when we examine the Civil Rights campaign. At this stage we shall concentrate on the charge of economic discrimination only insofar as it adds to the sense of communal solidarity and helps us to understand the nature of a divided society.

According to Richard Rose the economic gap between Protestant and Catholic was surprisingly narrow: 'Given their larger numbers in the population . . . there are *more poor Protestants than poor Catholics* in Northern Ireland . . .' (p. 289). Objectively, that statement is correct but does not add to our understanding of the conflict. Edmund Aunger takes it a stage further to argue that 'prominent occupational differences reinforced the religious cleavage, thereby providing an added barrier to reconciliation'.[22] Aunger's research reveals a three-way stratification between Protestant and Catholic occupations. Firstly, there is a marked tendency for Protestants to dominate the upper occupational classes while Catholics are found predominantly in the lower classes. Thus a Protestant is most often a skilled manual worker while a Catholic is most often a semi-skilled manual worker. Secondly, Protestants are concentrated in the higher status industries such as engineering while Catholics are disproportionately represented in the lower status industries, such as building contracting. Thirdly, within the same occupations and the same working contexts Protestants dominate the superior positions; and while a skilled craftsman may be a Catholic, it is more likely that his supervisor will be a Protestant.

Given this state of affairs in a closely knit society, it is possible to argue that Catholic sense of discrimination was heightened by everyday working experience. They saw that the better jobs went to Loyalists. They received their working orders from Protestant bosses or supervisors. They realised that the one lower status occupation dominated by Protestants, the police force, had a particular strategic significance. Only their university graduates did not experience any economic disadvantage. Most of them were members of the Catholic middle class whose existence 'may (in part) be attributed to the high level of segregation in Northern Irish society: this segregation creates the conditions which support the existence of a professional and business class whose role is specifically to satisfy the needs of their own religious groups'.[23]

All of this does not lead us to maintain that there was a sustained and overt discrimination by Protestants against the Catholic minority. After all, as Rose states, there were more poor Protestants than Catholics in Ulster, but Catholic self-perception was of a persecuted minority. Every act of the Government therefore could be perceived as an attempt to 'do down' the Catholics. It mattered little to them that a majority of their co-religionists lived in peripheral areas where there may have been difficulty in setting up industries. They did not understand that in a scarcity society their unemployment and their larger families made greater demands on the welfare state. The attitude of a Ballybeg Protestant summarises the miasma of distrust and ignorance that existed in this area:

> She was sure Catholics had no scruples about trying to abuse the Health Service and, indeed, that they felt politically virtuous in doing so – 'There's not a Roman Catholic in the country', she said, 'that hasn't two pairs of spectacles and false teeth.' Catholic doctors, she thought, were always ready to say a Catholic was sick even when he was healthy, if only it would get him government money.[24]

Catholic poverty was a result of their own fecklessness, and made undue demands on the welfare state. Protestant poverty . . . well, rather than see the authorities as the source of one's misery, it was better to lay the responsibility with the enemy within. That situation held until Catholic civil rights demands began being met: only then did Protestants begin re-examining their own positions.

Territoriality

> The very binary opposition between the two religious groups gives the individual an unusual degree of importance . . . Individuals were seldom isolated; almost everyone attended church and/or was a member of some political group, and they participated in many semi-social gatherings that had as their object the promotion of some religious or political cause.[25]

> I had heard a man from Co. Mayo say in South Armagh, when asked to give some opinion affecting social relationship, 'I'm only a stranger here.' Yet he had lived in our parish for about forty years.[26]

The sense of community in Ulster helps to explain the intensity of the conflict. Many of Belfast's nineteenth-century riots centred round a form of competitive localism. Territorial integrity was keenly felt and riots often occurred as a result of encroachment by the enemy: 'shatter zones', a kind of neutral battle area, were established. Recent events followed the same pattern. Thus, in the battle of the Bogside (1969) 'the fighting was always at boundaries represented by mainly mixed streets, or on the borders of separate Catholic and Protestant streets ... It sometimes looked as if both sides had agreed on certain battlegrounds and stuck to them'.[27]

People felt safer living among 'their own'. In Belfast, for example, in 1968 two thirds of the families lived in streets in which 91 per cent of the households were of the same religion. Often the degree of denominational interaction was minimal. Boal's research into an overwhelmingly Catholic area (98 per cent) and an equally homogeneous Protestant area (99 per cent) adjoining each other led him to assume the presence of two very distinctive territories. There was virtually no social interaction in Church and school attendance, grocery shopping and social visiting. Both read separate morning newspapers although the evening *Belfast Telegraph* played a useful role as a potential integrator across the religious divide.

Communities were virtually self-contained. Ron Weiner's description[28] of a loyalist community gives us some indication of why there was no need to move outside:

> It contained three primary schools, a playground, a Unionist Hall, 2 band rehearsal rooms as well as 70 shops and small businesses ... 4 public houses, three churches and three mission halls, all in an area with some 3,000 people. For many people therefore the community met all their needs and except for going on to the Shankill Road itself, they would rarely leave it.

Rural areas conformed to the same pattern. In Ballybeg there was a fairly clear segregation, with Catholics owning 75 per cent of the [poorer] hill farms and Protestants 65 per cent of lowland farms. The sale of land

> was more often directed to its symbolic worth than its monetary value. Ownership of a farm meant the symbolic occupation of an area. The transfer of a farm from a Protestant to a Catholic or vice versa was an issue that was emotionally more important if the townland in which the farm was situated had previously been owned entirely by the members of one faith.[29]

Nor was this simply a matter which exercised the minds of local farmers. A meeting in 1947 to raise funds to prevent Catholics from buying land at public auction was addressed by the then Prime Minister.

Local government

> The work of local councils ... cannot simply be judged ... from
> the way these bodies deal with drainage, health, education or the
> social services. Always overshadowing these pre-occupations is
> the larger question – is local government to remain in the hands of
> those who uphold the political settlement as it is now or to those
> who wish to destroy it?[30]

> We think that the situation which exists in local government will
> be more readily understood by American than by British readers.
> Many local councillors take it for granted that they are dispensers
> of patronage to their own side. ...[31]

Ulster's local government system fairly closely resembled the English
model. The Local Government (Ireland) Act 1898 was based on the
1888 and 1894 legislation for England and Wales. A clear distinction
was made between urban and rural districts but parish councils were
not created. Elections were held triennially and all but rural districts
had rating functions. They did not have the same responsibility for
protective services such as the police and civil defence, but in other
respects they fulfilled the same role as their British counterparts. By
1966 there were 73 local authorities.

Much of the politics of a divided society resides in local
government. Local councils allocated housing and as we have seen
with Ballybeg the symbolic occupation of property was important. It
was more than symbolic, however; property meant votes so that it
became essential to house 'your own'. Northern Ireland operated the
ratepayers' franchise (so that by 1967 there were almost 240,000 fewer
votes for local elections than Stormont elections) and the business-
men's vote, which allowed particular individuals a maximum of six
votes depending on the value of their property. That system had been
abandoned in Britain in 1945 when she reverted to universal suffrage
at local level. Unionist politicians considered that a dangerous
strategy lest some local authorities change hands. Local government
also meant jobs in a region of high unemployment. In 1970 local
authorities controlled 40,000 jobs. Charges of discrimination were
frequent: 'In the early sixties a person like myself could easily get a
place at university but would have been ineligible for a job as a
lavatory cleaner at Derry Guildhall, and that rankled.'[32]

'One man, One vote,' 'One man, One job,' became the civil rights slogans of 1968. They proved to be very effective because they were no more than simple British demands, and yet they struck at Unionism's Achilles heel. The Government had gone to inordinate lengths to secure local government control. Craigavon's regular forays among the people instilled a sense of pride and importance in local councillors. Their ability to house and, in some cases, find employment for their constituents was a tribute to the party machine. A letter from the Minister of Home Affairs to the Prime Minister dated 24 July 1934 shows that machine in action:

> The Derry Unionists find increased difficulty ... in getting suitable people returned to the Corporation and therefore they are promoting a scheme for the alteration of the Wards and reducing the number of members ... I have warned them that any publicity at the present time or speeches on the subject would only add to difficulties which I must always have in dealing with the alteration of Wards where the two parties are closely effective ... if proper steps are taken now, I believe Derry can be saved for years to come.[33]

'Proper steps' were taken with the redrawing of local boundaries in 1936. It amounted to a gerrymander. Gerrymandering was not necessary. Unionism could have lost Derry and other local authorities. It could have followed British practice after 1945 and adopted 'one man, one vote, one value' in local government. Its clear majority would have remained intact. But that was psychologically impossible. It still operated the client-patron relationship of nineteenth-century Orangeism. Its siege mentality was a fact of life. In a face-to-face society it had to be seen to be delivering the goods to its supporters, especially as the goods were a rare commodity. And it had to stand by its election slogan 'Not an inch'.

Conclusion

> ... it was an important aspect of the interrelationships of Catholics and Protestants in Ballybeg that all serious discussions of political and religious questions between them was socially forbidden. The result was their, at times startling, ignorance of each other's beliefs and practices....[34]

Protestants and Catholics had their own self-image and their own stereotypes. Neither corresponded very clearly to reality. That was not important. In a society where group solidarity meant so much one need not look outside one's own community for the 'truth'. Politics was about looking after 'your own' by maintaining your territorial integrity and group solidarity. The local government system seemed the best means to do that. We shall examine the implications of such a system later on. For the moment all we need stress is that given the lack of understanding at social level, political compromise at governmental level seemed very unlikely.

This book holds that community (Prot & Cath) self perception blurred reality and lead each to strongly held yet somewhat of an illusion as to their status.

4 A 'Majority Dictatorship'?

... there can be little hope for tranquillity in the political system if the electoral system, functioning normally, produces a majority in the legislature which rests upon a strong and disciplined large voting segment which will come together on all issues because its internal identity is stronger than any issue confronting it.

A. J. Milner[1]

Our attitude must be the attitude of the French to the Germans whilst France was under German occupation.

Eddie McAteer[2]

There are only two classes in Northern Ireland: the loyal and the disloyal. The loyal people are the Orangemen. The disloyal are the Socialists, Communists and Roman Catholics.

Unionist Backbencher[3]

The electoral system

The 1920 Act created a Parliament for Northern Ireland composed of a House of Commons and Senate. The lower house had 52 seats to be elected by proportional representation (PR). Section 14(5) of the Act made provision for the alteration of the electoral system after three years provided that the number of MPs remained the same and that in any redistribution of seats population was considered. Despite pledges to abolish PR at the first opportunity, it was not replaced by the plurality system until 1929. The most likely explanation for this delay was the presence of Britain's first (minority) Labour Government in 1924. Already the Labour administration had delayed the annual grant to the 'B' Specials, and some of its backbenchers expressed hostility to Unionist interests.

A comparison of the first two general election results illustrates why Unionists desired the abolition of PR. In 1921 they won 40 seats but lost eight of these in 1925, all of them in Belfast or its environs and all of them to candidates who belonged to the broad loyalist camp. Two members of the Government failed to get re-elected and no official Unionist headed the poll in Belfast. There the electorate seemed more interested in socio-economic than constitutional issues. By 1929, when the plurality system was first used, five of those seats had been recovered. Proportional Representation had allowed the electorate a measure of effective choice incommensurate with Unionist party ambitions:

> What I want to get into this House, and what I believe we will get very much under the old fashioned plain and simple system, are men who are for the Union on the one hand and who are against it and want to go into a Dublin Parliament on the other.[4]

Anti-partitionist representation had remained fairly stable in these three elections – 12, 12 and 11. Lord Craigavon's wish was a desire to thwart the growth of maverick Unionism. The monolith must be maintained.

After 1929, Ulster's elections settled into a predictable pattern. The Unionist party never secured fewer than 32 or more than 40 seats in every general election. Many seats were not even contested: between 1929–69 inclusive 37.5 per cent of the seats were returned unopposed, the vast majority of them being Unionist-held. Captain O'Neill, for example, first entered parliament in 1946 but did not face an electoral contest until 1969. The major parties gained from the revised electoral system, with the Unionists usually winning about three-quarters of the seats with slightly more than half the electorate's support. Two groups were seriously disadvantaged – independent Unionists and the Labour party: the former, for instance, took 29.1 per cent of the total vote in 1938 but won only three seats.

Stability implied inevitability. There was no getting away from the fact that the 'fundamental problem – at least for the Catholic minority – has been the *undeniable majority supporting the Unionist party*'.[5] Consequently opposition politics became sullen, plaintive and fragmented. This last point exposes the myth that PR inevitably produces a multi-party system. In the ten elections under the plurality system, four or five different parties always won representation at Stormont. 'In a tabulation of the results of the 1969 Stormont election, thirteen different party groupings were recorded – as well as three successful independents.'[6] Territorially, Ulster constituencies are small and local issues are important. Frustration among the opposition parties was inevitable, and the one-man party was an Ulster phenomenon. The Republican Labour party was an instance: '... Mr Diamond, the elderly Republican Labour member for Falls had in 1964 joined forces with Mr Fitt (then labelled Irish Labour) thus converting two one-man parties into one two-man party.'[7]

In 1973, after the imposition of direct rule, the British Government reintroduced PR for Ulster's elections. It wanted to fragment the Unionist monolith and to encourage voting across sectarian lines to help non-denominational centre parties. There had been only nine occasions (out of a possible 432) in the years 1933–69 when control of individual constituencies crossed the sectarian divide. But the transition to coalition politics so desired by British politicians has not come about. The idea that a new electoral system will bring fundamental political change proves to be an illusion.

In fact, ten new parties have emerged since 1970 – Alliance (APNI) Democratic Unionist Party (DUP), Irish Independence Party (IIP), Provisional Sinn Fein (PSF), Social Democratic and Labour Party (SDLP), Ulster Loyalist Democratic Party (ULDP), United Ulster Unionist Party (UUUP), Unionist Party of Northern Ireland (UPNI), Vanguard Unionist Progressive Party (VUPP), and the Workers' Party (WP). Since the UPNI is already extinct and the older NILP is virtually moribund, the centre ground is occupied by Alliance; it has never secured more than 14 per cent of the vote and is restricted to middle-class areas around Belfast Lough. On either side of Alliance the real battle goes on inside each community. The DUP and the UUP challenge each other for dominance of the loyalist community, whereas SDLP and PSF contest the anti-partitionist territory.

The party system

... Northern Ireland has a multi-party system operating within the framework of a dichotomous division about the Constitution.[8]

The party system in Northern Ireland today ... more nearly resembles the party system of a Latin American country, where military and foreign involvement in politics are taken for granted, or that of Weimar Germany or the first Austrian Republic between the wars when armed groups competed with parties for the power to rule.[9]

General elections were usually concerned with the constitutional question for Unionist governments conducted parliamentary politics in the belief that a section of the population were disloyal, and elections were meant to emphasise this dichotomy. Where possible elections were called at nodal moments in Ulster's history. 'Not an Inch' was the appropriate electoral slogan in 1925 at the general election called to confirm Unionist solidarity just before the Boundary Commission reported. In 1938 the Prime Minister considered it expedient to call an election shortly after Mr de Valera's constitution (1937) proclaimed *de jure* jurisdiction over Northern Ireland; and in 1949 after the Irish Republic left the Commonwealth. Similarly Unionist manifestoes emphasised the partition issue. A survey of leading articles in the (Unionist) *Belfast Newsletter* before every general election in the years 1929–58, concluded: 'The constitutional issue is not some piece of past history, now meaningless to the younger voters; it is continuously kept alive.'[10]

If one accepts that Unionists had a genuine fear that an anti-partitionist parliamentary majority would sweep Northern Ireland into a Dublin Parliament then one would conclude that they were justified in using free elections to highlight their opponents' disloyalty. Admittedly there were a few electoral irregularities – in 1967 there was still no impartial machinery to review parliamentary constituency boundaries and the university franchise was retained – but these were minor matters. Unionists had a clear parliamentary majority, and if an alternating two party system did not operate they could hardly be held responsible. Or could they?

Consider the case of the Northern Ireland Labour Party (NILP), cautious, conventional and most important, 'unionist'. At the 1958 general election it won four parliamentary seats and sought recognition as the official Opposition in an attempt to encourage the normal dialogue of parliamentary politics. The Government refused its request because, they argued, the Nationalist party was the largest opposition party. However, the Speaker granted it recognition. The Chief Whip, Brian Faulkner, candidly expressed Unionist thinking: 'The socialists have fought the election on one idea only, the need for a constitutional opposition . . . a more ineffectual opposition I cannot imagine . . . far more important their whole outlook seems to be alien to the Ulster tradition.'[11] Their request to assume chairmanship of the Public Accounts Committee was also refused on the dubious ground that, despite their willingness, it would be unfair to ask them to accept the burden of chairmanship as they were new to the House. In the next two parliamentary sessions Labour did attempt to raise the level of parliamentary debate and to operate the Westminster model. The Unionist party showed no interest in co-operating: rather it set out to destroy Labour.

In 1965 the NILP lost two of its four seats, much to the satisfaction of Terence O'Neill: 'The unfortunate Labour party, which in my predecessor's day had been gaining strength from election to election and which some sections of the press were forecasting would double its representation, was in fact practically annihilated.'[12] It was during the enlightened era of O'Neill with his public desire for normal politics that the decision was made to drive Labour beyond the pale. During the 1969 general election a Unionist party publication, *Northern Ireland Labour – What Are Its Real Aims?*, challenged Labour's loyalty. Much was made of the fact that in 1968 the NILP had helped establish 'The Council of Labour in Ireland', a body formed 'to enable joint consultations on social, economic and political issues without reference to partition'. That was enough for loyal Unionists: 'This move went further even than any taken by the Nationalist party in linking up with a political front in the Republic.' Furthermore the NILP 'has clearly shown evidence of its solidarity with Republicans, Communists and others ...'. The choice was a stark one: a steadfast Unionist party loyal to the British heritage and the advantageous economic link, or a suspect NILP allied to dark forces which must inevitably weaken that link.

Richard Rose's Loyalty survey indicated that only three parties, the Unionists, the Nationalists and the NILP, were specially visible to the mass of the electorate in 1968. One was covenanted with the protection of the Constitution, one was by definition disloyal, and the third had to be made suspect. Other parties were of no consequence: either they were 'extreme' or they had succumbed to the process of historical inevitability. (The Ulster Liberal party fitted the latter category. It collapsed between 1874–85 as much through its own venality and incompetence as to the challenge of the Home Rule crisis.) An examination of the major parties will add to our understanding of the nature of the division and help to establish the relationship of Ulster's political life to its party system.

The Nationalists

. . . we had a holding position.

Eddie McAteer[13]

. . . act stupid, demand explanations, object, anything at all that
will clog the Departmental machinery.

Eddie McAteer[14]

The Nationalist party was a party of failure. The partition of Ireland
in 1921 left it challenging Sinn Fein for the allegiance of a permanent
minority. The Nationalists were the remnant of the United Irish
League, John Redmond's party, which had been committed to
supporting Britain's war effort. Sinn Fein represented a more
militant strain – the men of 1916 – and captured more seats than the
UIL at the 1918 (Westminster) general election as a result of the
emotional anguish generated by the execution of the 1916 leaders.

When the first election to the new parliament was called in 1921,
the Nationalists were not prepared. Even with the aid of an electoral
pact with Sinn Fein, they accumulated 40,000 fewer first preference
votes, although both won six seats each. By 1925 the Sinn Fein star
was on the wane because its policy of abstention from Stormont on
principle disheartened Catholic voters who were beginning to place
more emphasis on social and economic issues than on Irish unity. The
Nationalists had won ten seats, Sinn Fein only two. By 1929 the Sinn
Fein threat had disappeared altogether.

In terms of parliamentary seats 1929 was the height of Nationalist
success; it won eleven Stormont seats. There was little possibility of
many more victories since only Catholics were canvassed: 'Beside
every name on the register was either an orange or a green mark. One
was pleased to turn over and discover a page with a preponderance of
orange marks. Such pages were easily done. Orange marks denoted
Protestants, and Mr McAteer did not send polling cards to
Protestants.'[15] The Nationalists, too, suffered from complete lack of
organisation operating as they did without a central headquarters or
paid officials, and (until November 1964) contesting elections
without a party programme. Half-hearted attempts were made to
construct the machinery of a proper parliamentary party in 1928 and
again in the 1940s. By the latter stage the party had lost its Belfast
base – there the Catholic working class was more inclined to vote for a

republican version of Labour – and was largely consigned to south
Armagh, south Down, south Fermanagh, much of Tyrone and Derry
city. The leadership was dominated by a rural Catholic middle class
without direction and without policy save the dream of a united
Ireland. It was, then, 'no more than a loose alliance of local notables
from different parts of rural Ulster',[16] open to the charge of being
clerically dominated: 'Its basic unit of organisation was not the
electoral ward but the parish ... Nationalist candidates were not
selected; they were anointed.'[17] In that respect the Nationalists
followed the lead established by Parnell in 1882 when he recruited the
Catholic clergy into his new National League, though it is probably
true to say that the clergy played little part in the affairs of the party
between elections.

Certainly the Nationalists relied much less on a sectarian
organisation than did the Unionists. The AOH played a significant
role between 1908 and 1921 when the party leader, Joe Devlin, tried
to create a powerful political machine by uniting the two organisations. Some of his colleagues objected to the alliance; they were
unhappy with the Hibernians' unsavoury image and sectarian nature.
After Devlin's death in 1934 the only prominent Nationalist to be a
member of the AOH was J. F. Stewart, leader of the party after 1958.
His successor, Eddie McAteer, declined membership because he
disliked the exhibitionism entailed in its marching in regalia, and he
was sensitive to Unionist accusations that the Order had undue
influence in the party. He did accept, however, that it was 'part of the
fabric for survival' since it could provide jobs for Catholics and
uphold their right to parade in certain areas.[18]

The Nationalists were also an 'opposition of principle ... bent ...
on ending once and for all the system on which the government
rests.'[19] We can best explain this aspect of Nationalism by examining
its parliamentary policy of intermittent abstentionism. Nationalist
MPs boycotted the first parliament completely but two of them took
their seats on 28 April 1925 before the Boundary Commission report
was leaked. By October 1927 all of them attended Stormont although
they were resigned to being an ineffectual permanent minority.
Except for the first election, when anti-partitionists put up 32
candidates and polled 32.3 per cent, the party was never in a position
to offer itself to the electorate as an alternative government. It was
reduced to a plaintive reiteration of old complaints. This attitude is

neatly encapsulated in a foreword written by Eddie McAteer to a booklet explaining the gerrymandering of local government in Derry:

> If you are robbed your indignation will receive general sympathy. If you are robbed every day people will weary of your complaints. It may even be that in time they will cease to believe you, because they will believe that no robber could possibly be so barefaced as to victimise you each day. Time and custom provide eventual justification for robbery.
>
> Every single day the Irish Nationalist majority in this Irish city are robbed of their elementary democratic rights.[20]

They managed to get passed only one piece of legislation – the Wild Birds Act (1931) – and contented themselves as acting as ombudsmen for their constituents. That was more than Sinn Fein could claim. It operated an abstention of principle and never had a representative at Stormont. By the 1950s a tacit alliance had been established whereby Sinn Fein contested Westminster elections and the Nationalists, Stormont elections.

The decision by the IRA to launch a campaign against Northern Ireland in 1956–62 was an embarrassment to the Nationalists. It was an untidy campaign which claimed the lives of six policemen and eleven republican activists or sympathisers, and failed as much because it received virtually no Catholic support as because of security vigilance. The futility of the campaign and the sterility of Nationalist parliamentarianism raised questions about the role of a Catholic opposition. Some Nationalist politicians were aware of a growing sense of frustration among the younger electorate. In 1962 Eddie McAteer suggested regular meetings between the AOH and Orange Order leadership in an effort to improve community relations. The 'Orange and Green talks' occurred between October 1962 and early 1963 but achieved no practical results.

Meanwhile the creation of a pressure group, National Unity, in December 1959 brought fresh ideas to minority politics. It stressed the need for unity and organisation among the opposition, and the doctrine that Irish unity could only be won through whole-hearted consent. The old attitude was to treat them as impudent upstarts. As a result, and after a series of abortive negotiations, a new party, the National Democratic party, was born in Belfast in 1964: '. . . the new party was electorally unsuccessful, but it did establish a number of

cardinal principles – a card-carrying membership, political organisation and a belief in constructive political action – that were seminal
influences on the SDLP in the first few years.'[21] Its very principles
were a fitting epitaph to the sterility of Nationalist politics. The events
of the late 1960s were to sweep the Nationalist party to one side. It is
difficult to quantify its achievement; perhaps it is enough to accept
that its role was simply to be that of a 'holding position'.

Labour

> Protestantism means protesting against superstition, hence true
> protestantism is synonymous with Labour.
>
> William Walker

> ... imagine what our situation would have been in the rest of
> Ireland if the only Irish socialist MP had voted against home rule.
>
> James Connolly

The above quotations encapsulate the dilemma for the democratic
socialist in Ulster. Connolly supported the merging of nationalism
and socialism to produce an all-Ireland labour movement. His
remark referred to Walker's attempt to be returned as a Belfast MP in
a Westminster by-election in 1905. The latter stood as a municipal
socialist proud of his achievements in Belfast and anxious to become
part of the British Labour movement. His candidacy failed and he
drifted out of politics. Connolly put his principles into practice,
committed his Citizens' Army to the 1916 rebellion in Dublin, and
was executed for his role in the affair.

Labour won three seats at the 1925 general election, a good result
considering that it withstood Nationalist accusations that it was a
parasite of Unionism, and Unionist taunts about its failure to deliver
a clear message on the border. Labour was often caught in that vice:
how to appeal to Protestant workers without alienating Catholics,
and vice versa. Individual candidates began pursuing their own
policy on the national question. Jack Beattie MP, for example,
adopted a strong anti-partitionist line in the 1930s, so that by January
1945 he had formed his Federation of Labour (Ireland) party. In
contrast, Harry Midgley MP moved from anti-partitionism in 1921 to
the establishment of his 'unionist' Commonwealth Labour party in
1942, the first non-Unionist in government in 1943, a member of the

Unionist party by 1947, and a Unionist Minister between 1949–57. Like the Nationalists they too were open to fragmentation. If we look at the party groupings of the Left which contested the 1945 election we find no less than 29 representatives of seven such groupings fighting the election – fifteen Labour candidates, one independent Labour, one Federation of Labour, six Commonwealth Labour, three Communist party, two Socialist Republicans, and one Derry Labour.

Labour, however, was in much better organisational shape than the Nationalists because the British Labour movement began giving it assistance after 1948, when the possibility arose that a few Ulster seats at Westminster might go Labour. Support did not imply a formal merger even after the momentous decision was taken to officially recognise the Union and to adopt the title Northern Ireland Labour Party in 1949. British Labour's contribution was to second an organiser to NILP, and to supply an annual grant to enable the party to appoint its first full-time secretary. Money was donated on a grant per seat basis to allow NILP to contest Westminster elections. So Transport House and NILP were fraternally close rather than formally affiliated.

NILP suffered from one major organisational defect, major, that is, for a party which claimed to represent the working class. The Trade Dispute and Trade Unions Act (NI), 1927, was not repealed in Ulster until 1968 – it had been repealed in Britain in 1930 – so that the 'contracting in' clause (whereby workers had to sign their agreement to paying a levy to the NILP) still stood. Consequently NILP did not enjoy the same financial advantages of the trade union connection as did its British counterpart. As well, the trade union movement was part of the partition game: in 1954 there were 68 British-based unions, 19 Northern Ireland unions and 5 Republic-based unions operating in Ulster. The latter, affiliated to the Irish Congress of Trade Unions based in Dublin, were not even recognised by the Unionist government until 1965. So while NILP had gained the support of some British-based unions this never amounted to more than 10 per cent of the province's total trade union membership, and must be contrasted with the 63 and 45 per cent claimed by the British and Irish Labour parties respectively.

Initially, the decision to support the Union was disastrous. In a highly polarised general election in 1949, in which Unionists made great play of the Irish Republic's departure from the Commonwealth and anti-partitionists received considerable financial support from across the border, NILP lost its two seats. The first signs of recovery occurred at the 1958 general election. Catholic radicals had grown weary of Nationalist procrastination and prevarication, while Protestant workers surveyed their declining economic prospects and plumped for NILP. They must also have approved of NILP's vigorous anti-republicanism as illustrated by the creation in 1957 in London of an Ulster Labour Group 'to counter the increasing flow of anti-partitionist propaganda into the British Trade Union and Labour movement and to further Northern Ireland's social and political interests therein.' In the general election there was a 6 per cent swing to Labour in the seven constituencies in which it stood, and it won four seats in Belfast. Three of its MPs were lay preachers.

It has been suggested that, after 1949, NILP was engaged in a consensus-forming strategy, the first stage of which was to break through into the Protestant community. The second stage was to consolidate that support, achieved in 1962 when it increased its overall support significantly in Belfast but failed to win more than its original four seats.[22] At this stage the strategy broke down. The intention was to woo Catholic support without losing Protestant votes. Nationalist seats were to be contested, and in 1964 the party proposed a private member's bill at Stormont to outlaw religious discrimination. It was NILP's first public recognition that such a practice was followed. But the party could not contain its contradictory support and split on the innocuous affair of Sunday swings.[23] Thereafter the party went into serious decline, losing two seats in 1965, a further one in 1969, reaching virtual extinction by 1979.

It may seem that we have paid undue attention to a party which was unsuccessful outside Belfast, was never represented at Westminster, never held more than four seats at Stormont, and at no time controlled any local district council. But we must remember that it was the party of Ulster's trade union movement, which, as we have seen, did not amount to very much, but which could lay some claims to non-sectarianism. More important, it attempted to work the Westminster model and introduced normality to Ulster politics. It was properly organised and had a socio-economic programme which looked beyond the basic constitutional question.

The Unionists

> The 'soul' of Unionism . . . is that Unionists, faced with a deadly external and internal threat, forget petty differences and unite on one great objective – the link with Great Britain. This means that the Unionist Party is quite unlike any other party in Britain. It is an umbrella, a common stand, a great crusading cause . . . When people face common danger, and a very real, ever-present danger, of absorption into the Irish Republic, the differences between Socialism and Conservatism pale into insignificance.
>
> John Laird[24]

> Our trouble was the Unionist party has always had far too wide an umbrella. You could hardly call it a political party because to be a Unionist all you were required to say was that you wanted to be part of the United Kingdom. You could really be any political complexion within that umbrella.
>
> Major James Chichester-Clark[25]

Since Unionism pervades virtually every aspect of political life in Ulster, a brief examination of the party's role can only be superficial. Already, in Chapter 1, we have examined the forces which brought it together. The Ulster Unionist Council (UUC) was formally constituted at Belfast's Ulster Hall on 3 March 1905. It relied on the Orange lodges and the local Unionist Club – there were 371 of these by 1914 – for grass-roots support. The combined ability of Edward Carson, the lawyer, and James Craig, the businessman, led it through the potentially treacherous third Home Rule crisis of 1912–14 and built up a formidable party machine. Its election returns for 1921 and 1925 illustrate the high and the low of Unionism's electoral performances. It never won more than 40 or less than 32 seats in the years 1921–69. Its all-time low of 32 in 1925 increased its sense of vulnerability.

A predominant strain in Unionism has always been its seeking after unity. Dissidents could not be tolerated and must be thwarted at the earliest possible opportunity. This overwhelming need for unity was seen as early as 1918 in the formation of the Unionist Labour Association: 'It is part of the duty of the Unionist Labour Association to expose the real aims and objects of Socialism and other anti-British movements,' proclaimed the UUC Annual Report (1926). Its purpose was to unite the Protestant working class to official Unionism in an age of abnormally high unemployment. Three of its members won seats at the 1918 (Westminster) general election and five were successful in the first election to the Northern Ireland parliament. J. M. Andrews, first Minister of Labour, future Prime Minister, President of the Belfast Chamber of Commerce, a large employer, and representative of Labour Unionism, personifies the nature of this unnatural alliance. As an effective organisation it had virtually disappeared by 1925 but it had served its role in these uncertain days. Only two of the hierarchy had a strong trade union connection at any time: Billy Grant, MP since 1921, a Minister between 1944–49, and President of the Shipwrights' Union for many years; and Harry Midgley, a former union official, who did not accept the Unionist party whip until 1949, although he was a member of the Government from 1942–57.[26]

The party's total supremacy in Ulster politics until the 1970s did not leave its leaders invulnerable. Only Lord Craigavon can be said to have secured the absolute trust of his party; he died in office in 1940. J. M. Andrews, his successor, was there for less than three years. He was held responsible for Ulster's somewhat tardy war effort and his choice of Government personnel, some of whom had been in office since 1921. Andrews was succeeded by Sir Basil Brooke in 1943, who was to be Prime Minister for twenty years. For most of that time Brookeborough (he was created a Viscount in 1952) was in firm control, but the growing unemployment problem made his last few years difficult. He resigned in 1963, to be replaced by Capt. Terence O'Neill, who never fully captured the trust of the party, facing crises of confidence in 1966 and 1967, and was forced to resign in 1969.

All the Unionist leaders were members of a 'squirearchy' leading a party which was predominantly working class. In this respect the party was not simply a mirror image of the English Conservatives – in fact it was more akin to continental Conservative parties which enjoyed the explicit support of a particular religious grouping. Even then comparisons with any western European political parties are invidious. None of them could call on the support of as powerful (and déclassé) an organisation as the Orange Order.

The real significance of Orangeism in the Unionist party is indicated by the fact that between 1921 and 1969 only three members of the Cabinet were not Orangemen on election, although another three left the Order while still in the Cabinet. (Significantly these resignations all occurred in the 1960s). Generally the party could rely on the Order:

> ... in a situation when every Prime Minister of Northern Ireland has been an Orangeman, where 95 per cent of all elected Unionist representatives in Parliament have been Orangemen, and where the Orange Institution is officially represented in the major organs of the Unionist Party it is clear that the ethos of Orangeism permeates the Party.[27]

That state of affairs was accepted by most Unionists since one in two or one in three of all male Unionist voters were in the Order.

But the Order did not rubber-stamp all party decisions. We have already noted the role of the Belfast County Grand Orange Lodge in the education dispute in 1923–25. Frank Wright records that in the 1950s and '60s 'it is widely reckoned that many lodges in the Shankill were predominantly Labour supporting. And on every occasion when explicitly *Protestant working-class* revolt against upper-class protestantism and unionism has arisen, the Orange Lodges have provided the major organisational structures to sustain it.'[28] From a Protestant fundamentalist perspective, Clifford Smyth has detected the evils of ecumenism in the Order: '... the Orange Order has still not completely clarified its position as to the ecumenical downgrade'.[29]

All of this suggests that the class alliance within Unionism may not have been quite as 'natural' as its allies believed, and that any idea of a deferential working class does not hold water in Northern Ireland. We shall see that from the early 1960s the Protestant working class began to take a more independent stance, and that in the 1970s the Unionist 'monolith' began to break up. That it held for so long can be explained by the historical circumstances which brought the party into existence in the first place and by the fact that the 'basic political problem of the poorer Protestant was that to secure his independence from the Irish Republic he had to support politically those whom he neither liked not trusted.'[30]

The divergent strains were always there. The presence of independent Unionists at Stormont between 1925–45, for instance, was not so much a threat to Unionism as yet further evidence of the personalism of Ulster politics. Eight Independents were returned in these years, although one, P. J. Woods, was elected to two constituencies in 1925. They tended to be people who had been spurned by the official party, only two of whom could be considered to be to the 'left' of the official party. With the abolition of proportional representation in 1929 and the reform of the Unionist party structure in 1946 the number of Independents dropped sharply.

A potentially more damaging threat was recurrent intra-Unionist disputes. J. H. Whyte[31] has made a study of the division lists to ascertain to what extent and on what issues Unionist backbenchers voted against the government between 1921–72. He concluded that most opposition came from the 'right', but that a populist strain emerged after 1929, combining right-wing suspicion of government extravagance and bureaucratic encroachments with left-wing demands that the government do more for the socially disadvantaged. Interestingly the largest number of dissidents featured in the first parliament – where there was no anti-partitionist opposition – when eleven backbenchers objected to the level of Ministerial salaries being awarded by the Government. Left-wing dissidents were few and usually represented Belfast working-class constituencies such as St Anne's, Woodvale and Shankill. The last two have been served by maverick Unionists or the NILP with the exception of one period in the 1950s.

Bew, Gibbon and Patterson explain these disputes in ideological terms.[32] They have traced the development of a populist sect within the parliamentary party from the 1920s. The populists wanted a more explicit sanction of popular Protestant self-assertiveness and local 'security', attempted to restrict the administration of the state to known loyalists, and believed in a policy of free spending, arguing that it was the Treasury's responsibility to bail Ulster out of any financial difficulties. At first the anti-populists, led by Lord Londonderry, Minister of Education, and J. M. Pollock, Minister of Finance, were in control but, with the waning republican threat after 1925 and continuing employment problems, the populists asserted themselves and the political leadership adopted an essentially demagogic role. The Prime Minister mirrored these strains: in 1921 he had made some effort to establish rapport with the Nationalists and the Catholic hierarchy, yet by 1932 he was asserting, 'All I boast is that we have a Protestant parliament and a Protestant state.'

Of course Craigavon was only too aware of growing divergences in the loyalist camp. The Local Option challenge had come and gone in 1929. Another one arose in 1938 when a Progressive Unionist party, disenchanted with the Government's housing and unemployment policies, put up twelve candidates against the official party. They all failed but took 30.9 per cent of the poll. A continuing low-key struggle went on between Belfast City Hall unionists and the party machine in Glengall Street. In 1935 the Corporation objected to having to levy a rate towards central expenditure on education; and in 1925 and 1942 the Corporation was charged with corruption and incompetence. In fact Stormont appointed three administrators in 1942 for more than three years to make all of Belfast's appointments, purchases and contracts.[33]

Outside observers have been quick to comment on the peculiarities of Unionism – a minor landowning aristocracy more content to lead the local hunt than to engage in dialogue with the cloth-capped, inarticulate Belfast worker. The leadership's public virtues – sobriety, steadfastness, narrowness and a certain degree of inarticulateness – helped to bind the alliance. It all appeared too much a caricature of late nineteenth-century Toryism. But it represented much more – an unhappy and unholy alliance of a people thrown together by what they were fundamentally opposed to rather than by any positive or co-operative principles. It is for that reason that we have not been concerned with the formal structure of the party, but simply to explain why the 'umbrella' held as long as it did.

Conclusion

On polling day the main concern of both parties was to minimise the inroads on their electoral strength likely to be caused by personation . . . Mr Fitt had publicly announced his precautions: a personation agent furnished with a list of 411 'Unionists' [i.e. Protestants] who had died since the register was compiled, would be stationed at each of the 102 ballot boxes in the twenty-six polling places.[34]

The above quotation refers to the contest for West Belfast in the 1966 (Westminster) general election. It explains the phenomenon of the 'dead vote', widespread personation by both communities in marginal constituencies. Although the overall result was inevitable, the keenness with which marginal seats were fought bore witness to the integrity of the quarrel. It was accepted that there was 'a majority' and 'a minority'. But the question always arose: 'Majority of what'? Since the fundamental problem concerned a population shaped by an artificial boundary imposed from without, it was essential for the beseiged majority to assert that it was an absolute majority throughout the length and breadth of the province, and for the minority to assert that this was not the case. Unionists were not allowed to forget that there were a number of local government areas containing Catholic majorities but under Protestant political control.

Permanent one-party rule inevitably raises questions about the quality of democracy in Northern Ireland. Arend Lijphart examines the proposition that Ulster was a pseudo and/or besieged democracy. He concludes (*vide* Marx's dictatorship of the proletariat) that it has been a majority dictatorship rather than a genuine democracy. His words are worth quoting at length because they explain so much of the nature of party politics and, especially, anti-partition politics in Northern Ireland:

> It is literally correct but nevertheless quite misleading to label the Catholic opposition as 'anti-constitutional'. Their opposition is not to the form of government but to the geographical contours of the political unit which the government rules. The anti-constitutional opposition is, therefore, not an anti-democratic opposition. Likewise, the Catholic opposition may be labelled as 'disloyal' . . . because its criticism is aimed at the entire system and not just at particular governments or parties. But in the Northern Ireland context, a disloyal and anti-system opposition is not necessarily an anti-democratic one. Therefore, instead of a weak democratic elite faced with an anti-democratic challenge, the Northern Ireland problem is more clearly one of a majority dictatorship dealing firmly with a minority claiming both democratic rights and a different political framework.[35]

5 A Devolved Administration

... the intractability of the 'Irish problem' and the uncomfortable lessons of history provided every inducement to the Government in London to keep Northern Ireland out of United Kingdom politics.

The Kilbrandon Report, para. 1303

... Though we do not breed as many Grand National winners as Eire, we turn out useful ships, machinery and linen.

Sir Walter Smiles[1]

By ... identifying the high degree of dependence of Northern Ireland on Great Britain, the system had tended to undermine to some degree the traditional self-reliance of the Ulsterman during the past half-century, thus helping to reverse the traditional contrast between Northerners and Southerners in Ireland.

Garret Fitzgerald[2]

Dublin

The Shadow of the Anglo-Irish Treaty signed on 6 December 1921 has hung over the politics of the island ever since. The acceptance of Dominion status by Michael Collins created a bitter cleavage which has been integrated into the political party system. The victory of the pro-Treatyites in the ensuing Civil War may have brought Ulster Unionism some comfort but not very much, since no-one at that time defended the 1920 settlement as anything more than a temporary compromise. The victorious Michael Collins believed it to be 'not the ultimate freedom that all nations aspire and develop to, but the freedom to achieve it'. His republican opponents objected to the Treaty on three main grounds: firstly, they were unhappy with partition, even in the short term; secondly, they disliked the fact that it was couched in the language of royalty and Empire; and finally they did not approve of Irish ports being leased to the Royal Navy. The last two objections were met when the Royal Navy relinquished all

Irish ports in 1938, and when Eire formally became the Republic of Ireland in 1949 and left the Commonwealth.

In the beginning W. T. Cosgrave, first Prime Minister of the Irish Free State, established a working relationship with Sir James Craig. Cosgrave's tough law-and-order approach and his conservative budgetary policy 'helped to consolidate the Civil War division by favouring the classes that had supported the Treaty at the expense of the poorer sections of the community from which the Republicans drew much of their strength',[3] and this won him some friends in Unionist circles. But there were other factors to offset this advantage.

Firstly, the legitimacy of the regime was not guaranteed. De Valera's supporters boycotted the new parliament, and although they acknowledged military defeat in 1923 they did not surrender their weapons. They entered the Dail in 1927 as the Fianna Fail party and formed their first government in 1932, leaving an estranged minority outside parliamentary politics who have posed an intermittent threat ever since. It was not until that 1932 victory when Cosgrave's Cumann na nGaedheal party handed over power gracefully that the legitimacy of the state was established. Sixteen successive years of Fianna Fail government underlined that stability.

Secondly, the nature of the new regime was not to Unionist liking. The Treaty debates had shown the ingrained anti-Britishness of the Irish Free State. In a more subtle form the adoption of Irish as the first official language widened the misunderstanding between the United Kingdom and Ireland. It has to be remembered that cultural nationalists had generated the battle for independence some decades previously, and it has been said of De Valera that the restoration of the language meant more to him than the restoration of the six northern counties. Cultural nationalism was little appreciated or understood in the United Kingdom. The British saw compulsory Irish indoctrination. In one respect they were correct:

It presented generations of children at school with texts, for example, which did not automatically reflect the fashions and clichés of the English-speaking world, but brought the pupils into contact with a world of ideas which was at once alien and, mysteriously, intimately their own. To some extent, Irish as a test served the independent State much as Protestantism as a test served the home rule province in the North.[4]

Thirdly, the 1921 settlement had not established economic independence. The Irish Free State lacked a proper industrial infrastructure.
Slightly more than half the population worked in agriculture, which
had a deplorably low level of productivity. By 1924 98 per cent of
Irish exports were going to the United Kingdom. And political
instability created economic uncertainty. Hence a monetary policy
which tied the currency to sterling and kept the Irish Bank Rate at 1
per cent above the current British rate to encourage capital to remain
in Ireland. Hence, too, the wooing of a *rentier* class which had
supported the Union. The government's heavy reliance on a
regressive taxation system and conservative monetary policy may
have halted the flight of capital initially but seems to have had little
real effect in the long term! '. . . a firm of American experts, called in
(in 1952) to analyse the Irish economy, came to the conclusion that
the country's dependence on Britain was so strong as to be
incompatible with the status of political sovereignty.'[5]

Government policy may have indirectly staunched the Protestant
outflow, but the fact remains that in the years 1911–27 the Protestant
population decreased by 32.5 per cent in the Irish Free State; the
comparable figure for the Catholic population was only 2.2 per cent
in the same period. In the longer term, the decrease in the Protestant
population from 11 per cent in 1911 to 4 per cent in 1961 increased the
notion of a religiously homogeneous state. Soon the epithet
'theocratic' was to be added. Catholic social doctrine became
embodied in the Constitution of 1937. That must be seen in its
historical context. De Valera believed that its 'first, central and
supreme purpose was to complete the national revolution and to
obtain the voluntary and firm declaration from the Irish people of the
independence and sovereignty of Ireland.'[6] It was essentially, then,
what John A. Murphy calls 'both a constitutional imperative and a
document of national philosophy'. Thus it claimed, under Articles 2
and 3, *de jure* jurisdiction over the whole island. Certain other
articles emphasised the Catholic ethos. The right of divorce was
forbidden; the family was recognised as a 'moral institution
possessing inalienable and imprescriptible rights, antecedent and
superior to all positive law'; and the Catholic Church was seen to
have a 'special position'. Other religions were specifically recognised
in the Constitution, whereas the Catholic hierarchy had demanded
that it should be the 'established' Church. Instead what was called its

'special position' became another example of de Valera's genius for the empty formula. It should be said, too, that it represented a fashionable, if ephemeral, trait: 'Indeed, it was hailed in some quarters as a tolerant and liberal document and proved to be a model for the constitution makers of Burma a decade later!'[7]

The 1937 Constitution is at the heart of the North-South conflict. Articles 2 and 3 are especially objectionable to the Ulster Unionist in that 'they make a territorial claim in the context of a Constitution which is otherwise Roman Catholic in spirit'.[8] Moreover its architect, Eamonn de Valera, had long been a particular bogeyman of Unionist demonology. He was a complex personality – the usual epithet used to describe him was 'jesuitical'. His vision of Ireland was so far removed from the conventional wisdom of twentieth-century industrial life that that in itself added to Northern misunderstanding of the Southern way of life: 'The Ireland we dreamed of would be the home of a people who valued material wealth only as the basis of a right living, of a people who were satisfied with a frugal comfort and devoted their leisure to the things of the spirit' (St Patrick's Day speech, 1943). His problem was to realise that rhetoric was not enough. By the early 1960s the Republic of Ireland lagged well behind Northern Ireland in all spheres of social welfare.

De Valera was essentially a revolutionary leader and a visionary who contributed greatly to the enmity between the two parts of the island. His obsession with the evils of partition took him around the political capitals of the world in an unremitting denunciation of the Stormont régime. It fed his followers a diet of heroic imagery and gave the Unionists a raison d'être. It was conducted at the cost of social progress in the South and communal peace in the North. The result of that rhetoric has been correctly analysed by a Dublin constitutional lawyer during the period of the IRA offensive of 1956–62. His words deserve to be quoted at some length:

> For thirty-five years our leaders have been waging a cold war against the North, and if the cold war has now become a shooting war, those who started and carried on the cold war must accept their share of responsibility. The policy of our leaders has been to coerce the North through the intervention of England, America, the United Nations or some outside power; the policy of the illegal organisations is to do the job themselves. You may call the former

policy a constitutional policy, and the latter a physical force policy, but both are basically policies of coercion. Both policies spring from the same presuppositions concerning the origin of Partition, both refuse to face the facts of the situation, and both are doomed to failure.[9]

The nineteenth-century Unionist stereotype of the Catholic Irishman survived Irish independence – priest-ridden and poverty-stricken. Continuing immigration from the South was balanced by a small increase in the Northern population. Official contact between both parts of the island diminished. Trade across the border was one example; it fell from £17 million in 1924 to only £5 million by 1937. But behind de Valera's idyllic pastoralism was hidden a real truth – the need for a frugal self-sufficiency. The policy of protectionism which emerged has produced an indigenous capitalism and a more diverse industrial base than that which existed in Northern Ireland. Economic development was helped 'by an approach to the role of State industry which was notably less doctrinaire than that of the Northern Ireland Government'.[10]

The accession to the premiership in 1959 of Sean Lemass created little stir in Northern Ireland. He was yet another 'man of 1916', admittedly more pragmatic and more technocratic. There appeared to be little reason to believe that the rules of the game needed to be altered. Fianna Fail would continue to make the right noises from time to time, but the walls of Stormont would not crumble. In fact, as we shall later, Lemass engaged in a policy of myth-destroying combined with sound economic planning. While Loyalist and Republican maintained their shared stereotypes, Lemass undermined the foundations: 'In the years 1960–73 Ireland enjoyed a growth in productivity (Gross Domestic Product per person employed) of 9.1 per cent, which was equal to that of the German Federal Republic and surpassed in the EEC only by France (9.9 per cent) and Italy (11.4 per cent). This compared with a growth in productivity in the United Kingdom of only 5.5 per cent.'[11] Politics in the Republic had become more concerned with economic planning than the empty rhetoric of the early years. A *de facto* convergence in the economic sphere between North and South was occurring. It was to have a profound effect on the politics of the island. Primordial sentiments were still strong but confidence in the integrity of the quarrel was disappearing.

London

> Northern Ireland was crammed into what was called the General
> Department, which was responsible for anything which did not fit
> into any of the major departments of the Home Office. It covered
> such matters as ceremonial functions, British Summer Time,
> London taxicabs, liquor licensing, the administration of State-
> owned pubs in Carlisle, and the protection of animals and birds.
> One division also dealt with the Channel Islands, the Isle of Man,
> the Charity Commission and Northern Ireland, and this group of
> subjects was under the control of a staff of seven, of whom only
> one was a member of what was called the administrative class.
>
> James Callaghan[12]

Callaghan's description of Home Office concern with Ulster affairs
prior to 1968 is an accurate account of the general irrelevance of
Northern Ireland in British statecraft. As early as 1922 a convention
was established at Westminster whereby Ulster affairs could not be
discussed on the floor of the House of Commons because Northern
Ireland had her own subordinate legislature: that convention
remained in operation until 1969. Richard Rose calculated that in the
five years preceding that date the Commons devoted less than one-
sixth of 1 per cent of its time to discussions of Ulster affairs, and most
of these were matters of trade.

On the security level Westminster appears to have given a free
hand to Stormont. We have already seen that in 1922 the British
Cabinet complied in paying the unpopular 'B' Specials. A better
example concerns complaints of police brutality in the 1932 Belfast
Outdoor Relief Riots from British trade union leaders:

> ... the Home Office felt it necessary to ask the secretary to the
> Northern Irish Cabinet for further information. But as the Home
> Office's C.M. Martin-Jones was careful to write, 'I intend to
> ignore the enclosed [Trade Union] correspondence' [PRONI Cab.
> 7B/207]. This tone of complicity is frequently to be found in the
> 1930s correspondence between the two Cabinets.[13]

Provided that the Ulster issue was not thrust before the general
public's consciousness, Westminster was more than willing to remain
aloof. In that respect the Ulster problem can be equated with the
Negro problem in the United States, where the federal system was

used as a device to avoid intervention as long as the states appeared to have everything under control.

Fiscal relations were much more complex than the general public in Ulster realised. We have seen in Chapter 2 that Stormont was to be given a comfortable income and left to its own devices. With the exception of agricultural payments, Westminster's control over Northern Ireland expenditure was slight, a situation which was exploited by the first Prime Minister at Stormont. It was soon evident that Northern Ireland did not have the resources to carry on an independent policy. This helps to explain why she adopted a 'step by step' policy with Westminster, and was unable to prevent the encroachment of socialist policy when Labour came to power after 1945.

Yet Northern Ireland had one distinct advantage over the remaining peripheral regions of the United Kingdom: she was not tied too closely to the centralising 'regional' policy of both major parties. Labour ideology favoured national economic planning and the development of social services under central control. This attitude changed with the publication of the Barlow Report in 1942. It suggested that it would be socially and economically more desirable to move jobs to the people rather than vice versa. In consequence the post-war Labour government pursued a vigorous regional policy, but its Conservative successors followed a more 'free-wheeling' policy towards the regions. Thus in 1952 the Minister of Supply, Duncan Sandys, told a Belfast audience worried about unemployment 'In the long run this is an Ulster problem which only Ulster can solve.' Equally, in 1960 a Westminster decision to offer increased incentives to industrialists to set up factories in British development districts detracted from the comparative attractiveness of Ulster's own scheme of generous inducements. Nonetheless Northern Ireland did have a head start. She had gained in the period 1947–59 when Westminster decided to stop building advanced factories on the mainland; and she was able to set up offices abroad to attract industry to Ulster whereas Scotland and Wales had to look to central government to protect their interests.

Benign neglect suited the Unionist Party, especially when the Conservatives were in office. However the return (in 1945) of a Labour Government raised fears again that Northern Ireland's constitutional position was in danger. Some Unionists even began considering dominion status to protect their interests, but their fears were soon dispelled. In fact, Labour strengthened the link when it passed the Ireland Act 1949. A much greater danger lay in the political implications of the development of the Welfare State. This undermined Unionist hegemony in a much more insidious manner because it slowed down the rate of Catholic emigration and raised the economic expectations of the Unionists' natural allies, the Protestant working class.

Belfast

In some respects Stormont was an exemplary model of a devolved parliament in practice. Its legislative output was respectable. 1968 was a typical year; it enacted 34 public statutes in comparison with Westminster's 77 public Acts of which the majority did not apply to Northern Ireland. The evidence suggests that 'a substantial part of Stormont's legislation was not of a kind which followed very closely that previously enacted at Westminster'. Northern Ireland's parliamentary draftsmen made good use of their limited resources and subordinate status by 'foraging in the Westminster statue book, selecting the best and improving on it in the light of some years' administration over the channel'.[14] Legislation dealing with the treatment of offenders is one example.

A more interesting area is the question of legislative innovation, and the lack of it. Stormont exercised its discretion by deliberately not legislating on such matters as divorce, abortion, capital punishment, homosexuality and personal finance, all of which had been the subject of legislation at Westminster. On the other hand, it passed legislation on matters peculiar to the province such as establishing a folk museum or giving loans to the Belfast shipyard. And it even acted as an innovator – wild birds were given legislative protection in Northern Ireland sooner than anywhere else in Britain.[15]

We must remember that Stormont was a half-time affair. Its Cabinet members were not overburdened: 'I remember Lord Brookeborough himself telling me that when he had been made Minister of Agriculture before the war he had been told that an afternoon a week would suffice for the discharge of his duties'.[16] But those conditions changed in the postwar world. Government was expected to intervene more and more to enrich the daily lives of its citizens. Unionist Ministers had, wittingly or unwittingly, propagated the idea that theirs was a sovereign parliament. Now their followers demanded evidence of successful action, and they were not entirely happy with the results. Ulster's record as a devolved administration was a contributory factor in its downfall in the 1970s.

Northern Ireland as a 'branch economy'

> Northern Ireland was born with a home market too small to support a diversified industry. Her industrial imbalance was of a peculiarly intractable kind. She had only two major industries, linen and shipbuilding, which at the end of the fifties provided about 40 per cent of the total employment in manufacturing industry . . . the Government of Northern Ireland has no control over trade with any place outside the six counties.[17]

The first Government inherited immense social and economic problems. Unemployment ran at 18 per cent in 1921; five years later it reached 25 per cent, the average rate for the next decade. Levels of unemployment have always been significantly above the United Kingdom average.[18] The reasons are many. Northern Ireland is less endowed with raw material and sources of power, and is more remote from the main domestic markets. She had a larger natural increase in population: 1935–46, 7.4 per 1,000 in Northern Ireland, 3.9 in Great Britain. She suffered severely from relative capital starvation. She had a preponderance of private firms over limited liability companies: 60 per cent in Northern Ireland in comparison to the United Kingdom average of 35 per cent. An abnormally large portion of the savings in the province was drawn off from the local markets into centralised institutions which tended to invest them in Government or industrial securities in Britain.[19] Finally there was a lack of industrial diversity. A. J. Brown has calculated 'co-efficients of specialisation' based on the distribution of employment in 1966. These show that Northern Ireland and the West Midlands were the most highly specialised of the eleven standard regions of the United Kingdom.[20] Consequently no substantial block of 'sheltered' industries existed when exports were bad. Additionally her staple industries continued to contract.

Linen and shipbuilding suffered from the exigencies of international competition, and agriculture from increased productivity, i.e. modernisation meant growing unemployment. Linen, which employed about one quarter of the industrial population in 1939, had reached its peak in 1927. The linen chiefs placed short-sighted gain in front of long-term rationalisation, so that a 15 per cent cutback in employment in 1954 followed a postwar boom. Thereafter linen was replaced by synthetic fibre. In shipbuilding employment figures fluctuated in the interwar years. By 1950 one in five of manufacturing jobs in Belfast were in that industry, but by that stage a steady decline in United Kingdom shipbuilding output had set in. The decline was very rapid in Belfast: between 1961–64 employment in shipbuilding and allied industries dropped by 11,500 or 40 per cent. Agriculture is a postwar success story. Output increased by 80 per cent between 1938–60, a factor explained by growing mechanisation – 350 tractors in 1939 grew to 30,000 in 1960. Unfortunately, increased efficiency meant rising unemployment, a drop of 28,000 (or nearly one-third) between 1950–60.

This serious decline in the staples had added to Northern Ireland's perennial unemployment problem. Ironically it was occurring at a time when the artificial prosperity induced by the increased industrial activity of the war had raised the Ulsterman's standard of living in the present and aroused his expectations for the future. A programme of industrial expansion became essential after 1945. However, its interventionist record in the interwar years is patchy: road transport had been nationalised in 1935, and the ailing shipbuilding industry received assistance from the Loan Guarantee Acts of the early 1930s. These actions contrast Craigavon's essentially non-doctrinaire approach to economic problems with the usual antipathy of Unionism to anything remotely resembling socialism.

All that changed after 1945 with the effort to attract foreign investment. The Industries Development Acts (NI) offered more generous inducements to industrialists than its British counterpart, the Distribution of industry Act (1945). This strategy began to pay dividends.

Between 1950 and 1969 at least 125,000 new jobs were created, widening the industrial base and greatly lessening the dependence on the traditional, but declining, sources of employment.... In consequence, the annual average rate of increase in GDP per capita during 1950–67 was 2.9 per cent in Northern Ireland and 2.3

per cent in the United Kingdom, while the productivity of labour grew by 49 per cent in Northern Ireland and by 26 per cent in the United Kingdom.[21]

State intervention heralded the economic decline of the indigenous middle classes. The Unionist leadership represented a narrow class interest: 12 of Belfast's 14 Unionist MPs in the 1950s were either proprieters or managing directors. Their interests were represented by the Minister of Commerce, Sir Roland Nugent, who complained: '... there seemed to be a feeling that the government in their efforts to attract new industries were overlooking the necessity for encouraging and helping existing manufacturers'. His words were not unheeded. The Re-equipment of Industry Acts (1951–62) provided for the payment of grants towards expenditure incurred in the re-equipment or modernisation of industrial undertakings, but did not stipulate that increased employment was a necessary prerequisite to qualify for a grant.

Another effect of government intervention was to alter the nature of employment. A major area of growth was the service sector. During the 1950s it increased by 18,500 as a result of government investment in education and welfare services. Interestingly this is an area in which Catholic employment is significantly high:

The patterns of male involvement in the services sector show almost two-thirds of Roman Catholic men in this area of the economy whereas just over half of Protestant men are in this category ... Roman Catholics tend to be disproportionally represented in education and health and welfare services, while Protestants are disproportionally represented in finance and industry....[22]

The political implications of this shake-up in Northern Ireland industry were manifest. In 1958, when unemployment in Belfast rose by almost 50 per cent, the Northern Ireland Labour Party (NILP) won four Unionist seats in the capital. They were to retain these in 1962 and increase their share of the poll. In 1961 and 1962 mass protest marches were held in Belfast as threatened redundancies mounted. 20,000 (mostly Loyalist) workers demanded Government action against unemployment in a Belfast protest in March 1961. The traditional May Day march drew more support than at any time since the First World War. By July unemployment stood at over 7 per cent in Northern Ireland in contrast to the United Kingdom average of 1.2 per cent. 1962 saw the same pattern with a NILP demand for the recall of Stormont in the summer attracting 100,000 signatures. There was considerable unrest on the Unionist backbenches. Frank Wright has correctly summed up the period:

> . . . in the situation that developed in the late 1950s and reached a peak in 1963, where workers in the skilled trades were increasingly becoming victims of redundancy, the percentage of protestants amongst the unemployed probably rose considerably. The greater this tendency the less plausible it becomes to represent the unemployment issue as a 'Catholic' problem, and the more authentically it becomes a 'class' problem, common to protestant as well as to Catholic workers. In the 1930s under similar conditions, Unionist leaders had combatted this situation by giving the appearance that they were doing something about *Protestant* unemployment. Now, in the 1950s and 1960s, such tactics were no longer viable, if for no other reason, for fear of attention from the outside world.[23]

That is not to say that Lord Brookeborough, was not capable of attempting the old tactics: 'Ulster has only room for one party . . . recent economic issues should not divide Protestants.'[24] But it was no longer possible to conceal the fact that the Unionist Government were prisoners of Conservative ideology. The 1950s were a decade of to-ing and fro-ing between Belfast and London. Most of the traffic was in one direction and invariably Unionist ministers returned with empty pockets. Northern Ireland did not feature prominently on the Conservative horizon. Captain O'Neill recalls one visit he made to the Prime Minister, Harold Macmillan: 'He was, however, surprised that I wanted to talk about anything other than the weather.'[25] The provincial Parliament needed to look to its own resources, and it is here that its record was so dismal.

Housing

> Despite the British record going back at least to the Town and Country Planning Act of 1947, no planning of any kind was even considered here until 1960, when Sir Robert Matthew was commissioned to prepare a regional survey of Belfast. Professor

Thomas Wilson followed with a more general study three years later ... in much the same way in which the Minister of Labour *Reports* in 1934 finally impressed upon Whitehall the magnitude of the depression in industrial Britain, the Matthew and Wilson reports brought to the attention of the leadership at Stormont what should have been evident after a cursory stroll around Belfast: the area was dirty, crowded, and aesthetically displeasing...[26]

Ulster's first housing survey was carried out in 1943. It was estimated that 97,000 new houses were needed more or less immediately. There were many reasons for the shortage. Wartime bombing destroyed 3,200 dwellings; and there were certain technical difficulties:

> The amount of work connected with obtaining [planning] approvals is rather more than in Great Britain ... The cost of building in Northern Ireland is higher ... a large proportion of material and equipment must be imported from Great Britain. The contracting capacity of the Province also is not great.[27]

But that is very much a partial explanation. Fundamentally Government policy between the wars did not reflect a recognition that the state was responsible to provide adequate housing for the whole population. Northern Ireland had not followed British housing legislation of 1924, 1933 and 1935 which provided for increased local authority involvement in housing and in slum clearance. During the period prior to 1881 and up until 1970 only 12 per cent of the housing stock had been built in the interwar years. Local authorities were the worst offenders in these years. Indeed, even when the gravity of the situation was apparent the Minister of Health and Local Government had to write to Belfast Corporation in 1960 complaining about its building record and pointing out that only a small share of the city rates was going to housing.

The postwar record is much more respectable. In February 1945 a statutory body to supplement the local authority housing programme, the Northern Ireland Housing Trust, was established. It began with a considerable disadvantage in 'the fact that the Trust faces entirely postwar costs, having no prewar assets in the form of completed estates or purchased land, as many local authorities in this country enjoy...'[28] If parity was being chased then the postwar rate of building would be acceptable, but since so much leeway had to be made up housing continued to be an awkward political problem.

Despite the civil rights slogans of the late 1960s we should not assume that it was an entirely Catholic problem. The following descriptions by the Belfast Medical Officer of Health in March 1973 refers to an area of the loyalist Shankill in which 95 per cent of the houses were substandard:

> the dwelling houses in this area were built between 1852 and 1887. There was a state of general decay, disrepair, general dampness and instability. Many houses have no secondary means of access necessitating the delivery of fuel and the removal of house refuse through the dwelling. Amenities for personal hygiene were almost non-existent and very few houses have internal W.C.s. There was inadequate provision for the preparation and cooking of foods and, in many cases, improvised sculleries had enclosed the drains and obstructed lighting and ventilation....[29]

Only when it appeared that the authorities were improving Catholic housing conditions did Protestants begin to look closely at their own environment. Yet again the Unionist class alliance was put under severe strain.

The welfare state

> In our own case our powers are already much too great for the role of a modern subordinate government, but not great enough for a Dominion. Hitherto the difficulties have been masked by the fortunate accident that both Governments and both electorates have been in complete agreement on all major issues of policy, so that 'face' could be saved by the ingenuous device of 'step by step'. It seems doubtful whether we shall still be able to linger in this pleasant but quite illogical, half way house ... We must very soon decide which way we are going, 'back to Westminster' or forward at least another step towards Dominion status.[30]

The Government of Ireland Act did not mention the question of parity in the social services. Where it was possible Northern Ireland tried to provide the same social services as on the mainland on the principle proclaimed by Sir James Craig in 1922 that it would not be said 'that the workers in our midst worked under conditions worse than those across the water.' But it was not always feasible: parity of unemployment benefit, for example, was conceded in the interwar years only after strong trade union representation.

With the accession of the Labour Government in 1945 'step by step' in the social services became paramount. During the early months of 1946 a discussion took place within the Cabinet on what would happen if Westminster attempted to impose socialist legislation on Northern Ireland; hence the above memorandum. Papers were also presented by Mr Brian Maginess, Minister of Labour and Rev. Robert Moore, Minister of Agriculture. Options ranged from integration to 'that which has been adopted in the British Commonwealth, a gradual increase in the powers of the subordinate governments, partly by agreement, partly by constitutional convention and partly by statute' (Sir Roland Nugent). Some backbenchers entertained the idea of Dominion status. Unionist difficulties were expressed by Brian Maginness when he warned that 'if the Government is going to act merely as a trailer attached to the Great Britain motor there can no longer, in Northern Ireland, be a distinction between the Unionist and the Labour Party for the Union Party would, in fact, be carrying out a socialist programme'.

That is precisely what happened when earlier apprehensions with the Attlee Government dissolved: '. . . at Westminster the Unionist representatives joined with the Conservative opposition in resisting the socialist legislation which established the welfare state, while at Stormont the Unionist party solemnly resolved to annex as much of this legislation as possible to its own purposes'.[31] The principle of general parity between certain social services was provided for in the Social Services Agreement of 1949 which dealt with National Assistance, pensions, the Family Allowance, unemployment benefit and the Health Service.

This Agreement had two curious results. One was that the annual King's Speech at the opening of Parliament frequently 'made no mention of important legislation to come, because the party in power in Great Britain had not yet shown its hand', but was 'an anaemic document, full of platitudes for the past and pieties for the future'.[32] Secondly, Unionists learned to live with their schizophrenia. Their anti-socialism was demonstrated in the Conservative lobbies at Westminster, whereas their Belfast counterparts accepted socialist measures to defeat Northern Ireland's socialist party, the NILP. This considerable feat is explained in a party document, *Ulster is British: A Re-Affirmation of Ulster's Political Outlook*. Among other things it explains that the NILP's lack of success at the 1949 general election arose because 'the "man in the street", realising that Ulster's economy is closely knit and inter-dependent with that of Great Britain, could not support a Party, that would by its indecision constitutionally, jeopardise his employment and weekly income'.

In fact 'parity' has never worked in practice. The British Legal Aid Scheme (1949) was not implemented in Northern Ireland until 1965. Housing and health services have operated differently in Northern Ireland. The disparity in the latter has been Ulster's gain because a much higher sum per capita has been made available for new hospitals and hospital modernisation in Northern Ireland than in Great Britain. There was one exception to this rule. The British National Health Service Act (1946) included the 'Stokes' clause designed to enable hospitals with religious links to maintain their character within the National Health Service. This clause was excluded from Northern Ireland's legislation of 1948, so that the largest casualty hospital in North Belfast, the Mater Infirmorum Hospital, with its close links with the Catholic Church, remained outside the scheme. Another example was the abortive attempt by the Unionist Government in 1956 to abandon parity in family allowances by reducing payments to large families, a proposal with clear religious overtones. Given these examples – and others could be added – it is difficult to disagree with the statement that the

British model of the Welfare State has operated in Northern Ireland to serve ends other than those of redistribution or meeting social need . . . Social services in Northern Ireland on the contrary have actively contributed to the deepening of political and social divisions and the polarization of communities.[33]

Conclusion
Most explanations of the Ulster crisis stress Catholic dissatisfaction and Republican agitation. Undoubtedly these factors are very important, but they do not tell the whole story. Years before the first Civil Rights march the Loyalist working class took to the streets in protest against social and economic conditions. Much of their

frustration belonged to devolution mythology. As 'loyal' British subjects they could not understand why their part of the kingdom did not enjoy the same affluence as Britain. The politics of the welfare state raised the question of relative deprivation. What was the sense of having a government at Stormont if it could not maintain the same welfare levels as the mainland? And why should welfarism discriminate in favour of the 'disloyal' Catholic?

Government could not publicly answer these questions. It was beginning to realise the true nature of the responsibilities attached to a devolved administration. It was a suppliant in need of outside investment and yet protective of its own local industry. It was a subordinate executive supported by those who believed it to be sovereign. And it had gone beyond the heady days of protecting its border from an external enemy. The politics of the Republic were more concerned with cash flow than guerrilla rhetoric. Ulster had to come to terms with the modern world.

6 One Man One Vote

What kind of Ulster do you want? A happy and respected Province, in good standing with the rest of the United Kingdom? Or a place continually torn apart by riots and demonstrations, and regarded by the rest of Britain as a political outcast? As always in a democracy, the choice is yours.

Terence O'Neill[1]

I should have fought O'Neill the election before I did, then perhaps the Ulster people would have been awakened sooner, or at least the brake would have been put on his treachery. O'Neill was the man who paved the way for Ulster's undoing.

Rev. Ian Paisley[2]

A state without the means of some change is without the means of its conservation. Without such means it might even risk the loss of that part of the Constitution which it wished the most religiously to preserve.

Edmund Burke

Terence O'Neill

The official version of Ulster is rooted in the late nineteenth century: a land of practical people engaged in heavy industry for the glory of the Empire. Their symbols were to be found in Belfast shipyards:

Down there at the end of the melancholy lough
Against the lurid sky over the stained water
Where hammers clang murderously on the girders
Like crucifixes the gantries stood.[3]

They were a puritan people who had little time for the arts: 'Wratin' poetry don't drave no rivets, yoong man,' V. S. Pritchett was told by a shipyard owner in the 1920s. It was not simply that the arts represented a needless diversion; they could be dangerous. Hence when Sam Thompson, a Belfast playwright, tried to stage *Over The Bridge*, his account of sectarian troubles in the shipyards, in Belfast in

1960, CEMA (the predecessor of the Arts Council) objected and withdrew its grant. Thompson responded by showing it elsewhere in the city and by describing Northern Ireland as 'the Siberia of the arts'.

The previous chapter has demonstrated that that self-image was being challenged by the harsh realities of economics. The decline in employment of 106,000 people since 1950 of the three staple industries spoke for itself. If any simple souls still doubted the reality, all illusions were stripped by the publication of the Hall Report (Cmnd 446) in October 1962. It was written by senior officials from relevant United Kingdom and Northern Ireland departments and was concerned with the continuing unemployment problems. It offered no real solution save encouraging the growth of new industries rather than subsidising further the inefficient staple industries. Its pessimistic outlook could be found in para 224 when it urged that 'further steps should be taken to find employment opportunities outside Northern Ireland and to induce unemployed workers to avail themselves of them'. In other words, Ulster workers were to become the *Gastarbeiter* of the uncertain British market. The Report has been described as 'a shock and a stimulus,' a euphemism which even Lord Brookeborough saw through. After undergoing an operation for a duodenal ulcer, he retired in early 1963.

His successor was Terence O'Neill. He emerged through the same consultative process used to choose the Tory party leader until 1965. Like Lord Home, he was the last party leader to be chosen in this manner. O'Neill's accent betrayed his background; he was a product of Eton, the Guards and the 'Big House.' His predecessors had known wealth too but they did not have the same family lineage as O'Neill. Moreover they were political patrons *par excellence.* Craigavon was the man who had 'distributed bones' and had made an art of patronage. Andrews was the large mill-owner and squire of the small village of Comber. He made it his business to know his workers and to endow their favourite past-time, cricket. His world-view did not extend much beyond his village: after he had had an audience with Churchill at the height of the Second World War, the British Prime Minister summoned his officials demanding to know, 'Who, what or where is Comber?' Brookeborough had been a founder of the 'B' Specials, a man who had walked the land with his tenants to prevent IRA incursions in the 1920s, and whose tragedy, according to his successor, was that 'he did not use his tremendous charm and his deep Orange roots to try and persuade his devoted followers to accept some reforms'.[4]

O'Neill did not have many 'devoted followers'. He was Olympian, a man of destiny who found the company of world leaders more convivial than those of his colleagues. (It will not have escaped his notice that on the day he resigned from parliament, another 'great man', General De Gaulle, resigned also). In mitigation it has to be said that it cannot have been easy to work with all his colleagues. O'Neill did not enjoy the endorsement of his predecessor, he had had to rely on a 'kingmaker', (the Chief Whip, William Craig), and he had to work closely with a powerful and embittered rival, Brian Faulkner. His style and his policy were in sharp contrast to those of Brookeborough. He considered that Cabinet members should work full-time and immediately drew up a Code of Conduct (much like Churchill's after 1951) which precluded some extramural activity by his Ministers. The Code was not universally popular with men grown used to the 'graceful' ways of Brookeborough, and, in fact, was used to remove his Minister of Agriculture, Harry West, in 1967. He gave the impression of being aloof, a trait which was not admired in a small province.

He did not always appreciate the need to explain his actions. The removal of his Leader of the House in 1965, the demotion of his powerful Minister of Development, William Craig, to the Ministry of Home Affairs in 1966, and the sacking of Harry West in 1967 inevitably offered hostages to fortune. He felt the need to ask his colleagues for a vote of confidence in April 1965, and in 1966 and 1967 'there were two revolts within the Unionist Parliamentary Party which O'Neill put down by the expedient of broadcasting to the people and challenging his opponents to put their case. This they were not willing to do and both revolts ended in votes of confidence of specious unanimity for O'Neill'.[5] His record as a constituency MP was not particularly noteworthy. Rev. Ian Paisley, his successor as MP for Bannside, catches the appropriate populist drift in this criticism: 'A man beneath contempt who talked of progress and who every day on his way to Stormont passed by 200 houses with no water and never thought to do anything about them.'[6] Men of destiny may have feet of clay.

Personality and style cannot explain the whole man. Vanity and touchiness are not qualities peculiar to O'Neill. His failure – if indeed it was failure – lies in his policies. His premiership has been noted for two interdependent themes: improving community relations and broadening Ulster's economic base. To succeed he needed to engage in a campaign of propaganda since the kind of Ulster he wanted clashed with the official version. In the right company he was strong on exhortation – speaking to a denominationally mixed professional audience, he could urge them to 'be united in working together – in a Christian spirit – to create better opportunities for our children'. But the exhortation of the Anglo-Irish ascendancy could not compete with the more raucous chorus of traditional Ulster:

> I am Ulster, my people an abrupt people
> Who like the spiky consonants in speech
> And think the soft ones cissy; who dig
> The *k* and *t* in orchestra, detect sin
> In sinfonia, get a kick out of
> Tin cans, fricatives, fornication, staccato talk,
> Anything that gives or takes attack,
> Like Micks, Tagues, tinkers' gets, Vatican.
> An angular people, brusque and Protestant,
> For whom the word is still a fighting word,
> Who bristle into reticence at the sound
> Of the round gift of the gab in Southern mouths.
> Mine were not born with silver spoons in gob,
> Nor would they thank you for the gift of tongues;
> The dry riposte, the bitter repartee's
> The Northman's bite and portion, his deep sup
> Is silence;[7]

Traditional Ulster came to be represented by Rev. Ian Paisley, another 'man of destiny.'

Modernisation
The Prime Minister's grand strategy presupposed the building of modern industrial infrastructure. To do so he needed to dismantle a nineteenth-century edifice. Besides the fact that she had her own bicameral Parliament and sent twelve MPs to Westminster, she also possessed 73 directly elected bodies, 24 statutory committees and 30 joint authorities or specialised bodies all drawing on the limited funds to serve a population of 1,500,000. Corporate decisions were not

easily reached. Responsibility for the main road systems in Greater Belfast, for example, was shared between the Ministry of Commerce, Belfast County Borough, Antrim and Down County Councils, seven Municipal Boroughs and five urban districts. A streamlined system was a major priority.

O'Neill was fortunate in inheriting the findings of the Matthew Commission (Cmnd 451, 1963) appointed in 1960 to draw up a plan for the Belfast region. The Report – *Belfast Regional Survey and Plan: Recommendations and Conclusions* – was attempting 'simultaneously to *demagnetise the centre* and reinvigorate the many attractive small towns in the region. 'Stop-line' and 'growth-centre' became the Matthew keywords: the former imposed a boundary around Belfast urban area to restrict the amount of land available for future development, and to persuade people to move to the latter, (seven growth centres named by Matthew and a new city to be created by linking the twin towns of Portadown and Lurgan). To co-ordinate this activity a new Ministry of Planning and Development was suggested to enable central government to be responsible for planning at the expense of the local authorities.

Matthew begat Wilson – *Economic Development in Northern Ireland* (Cmnd 479, 1965). The Wilson Report accepted the Matthew growth-centre strategy, set a target of 12,000 new houses per annum to be built by 1970, an employment target of 65,000 new jobs, and suggested the provision of training facilities to create a pool of skilled labour. Other commissions were in the pipeline. The Benson Report on Northern Ireland's railways (Cmnd 458) was published in July 1963; it advised that the railway system should be streamlined in much the same way as Lord Beeching suggested in Britain. An examination of higher education facilities in the province led to the publication of the Lockwood Report (Cmnd 475, 1965) which recommended the building of a second university in the little town of Coleraine, 72 kilometres from Belfast.

In the meantime a Ministry of Development had been established in 1964. A year later the New Towns Act (NI) created the new city of Craigavon and eight other growth centres. Ulster appeared to have entered a dynamic period of growth. When O'Neill had become Prime Minister, the province's first motorway was being constructed, a new airport had been built, and Altnagelvin Hospital, believed to be the most modern in Europe, was completed in Derry. The last great structural reform to be undertaken, the reform of local government, would complete the revolution. All of this would ensure that Ulster would enter a period of prosperity. To complete the circle – and ensure O'Neill's place in history – relations between the communities were to be improved.

The era of good feelings

... O'Neill's 'era of good feelings' was not a myth. A majority of Protestants and Catholics in all kinds of localities agreed that relations were improving in the period [of O'Neill's premiership] and very few anywhere thought they were getting worse. This suggests that Protestants and Catholics regard better inter-faith relations as mutually beneficial, and not a situation in which improvements for Catholics mean worse conditions for Protestants. There is nothing irreversible in such a trend.[8]

When Terence O'Neill became Prime Minister unemployment stood at 11.2 per cent. By April 1966 he could boast that the previous month's unemployment figures were the lowest for March since the war. Catholic attitudes towards the Stormont regime appeared to be more positive. We have seen that their emigration rate decreased in the 1960s and that they appeared to benefit from the new industrial strategy.

Catholics lent little support to the IRA's 'border campaign' of 1956–62. Admittedly they had voted heavily for Republican candidates in the 1955 Westminster election, but that may have signified just as much dissatisfaction with Nationalist party indolence as with the Brookeborough government. By 1959 – when the IRA offensive was in full flood – the percentage of the poll for Republican candidates had dropped from 23.7 to 11 per cent. Certainly, when the campaign was called off in February 1962 the IRA had faced reality: 'Foremost among the factors motivating this course of action has been the attitude of the general public whose minds have been deliberately distracted from the supreme issue facing the Irish people – the unity and freedom of Ireland.' There had been some skirmishes between Catholics and the RUC in Derry and Fermanagh in 1951 and 1952, but the last major intercommunal riots had occurred in Belfast in 1935.

During the 1950s Conor Cruise O'Brien worked as a civil servant in Dublin. When Sean Lemass became Prime Minister O'Brien remembers being sent to

> convey to various nationalist/anti-Unionist/Catholic leaders and publicists the wish of . . . the Dublin Government that they should take a more active part in public life, cease to boycott local official ceremonies, and associate with Protestants to a greater extent. Most of them heard me with resignation, but without manifest assent.[9]

Lemass encouraged dialogue by granting *de facto* recognition to Northern Ireland at an Oxford Union debate in October 1959. One year earlier a gathering of Catholic members of the professions 'crystallised the feeling that Catholics should be allowed to participate in public life without prejudicing their ultimate aspiration to Irish unity'.[10] This was to be the central political tenet of the new generation of Catholic democratic politicians who emerged out of the civil rights campaign a decade later.

To appreciate these changing attitudes we must look to the outside world for a clue. Catholic self-confidence grew because the era saw the regime of Pope John XXIII (1958–63) and the presidency of John F. Kennedy (1960–63). Pope John provides the *entrée*:

> . . .the Johannine translation of the concept of community from ideal to real terms seems to have been extremely important. It raised a very nasty problem for the Unionist leadership: their Catholic subjects . . . now began to demand that as members of a community they were entitled to expect the just rights of all members of that community. The very arguments that John XXIII himself had made so tellingly in the context of racial segregation had every relevance to religious *apartheid*.[11]

John offered simplicity and humanity in contrast to the cold formality of his predecessor. His calling together the Second Vatican Council encouraged the ecumenical spirit and a period of self-criticism within Catholicism. With John as Pope the Church appeared less monolithic and Catholics grew in self respect. When he died in May 1963 the flag was lowered to half-mast on Belfast City Hall. Kennedy's contribution was that he became the first Catholic President of the United States. His election as an Irish-American increased Catholic interest in politics in general, particularly since

Capt. O'Neill made a 'ludicrous and fruitless attempt to lure the illustrious Mick in the White House to pay a call on Stormont'.[12] This growing self-confidence could be seen on Catholic parlour walls in the 1960s when the spiritual and the temporal were represented by the triptych of Pope John, the Sacred Heart, and President Kennedy.

The communications revolution added to Catholic awareness of the outside world. After television broadcasting began in the province in 1954 the number of licences increased nineteenfold in eight years. The 'need for balance' was the dominating theme of the broadcasters. BBC radio had been concerned since 1948 with promoting a policy

> aimed at building a political consensus in a divided society. The policy involved accentuating the positive in community relations, stressing that which was held or suffered in common. Documentaries or feature programmes ... dealt with common problems and ignored the sectarian divide.[13]

That which was considered 'negative' – for example a series of *Tonight* programmes by Alan Whicker, critical of aspects of Stormont policy – was banned in 1959. Nevertheless, television did open up one's understanding of the other man's situation, and may have encouraged greater empathy. Another potential integrater was the province's only evening newspaper. Under the editorship of J. E. Sayers, the *Belfast Telegraph* switched roles from being a subservient echo of traditional Unionism to that of critical supporter of O'Neillite policies.

Finally, Catholics were encouraged by the return of a Labour government in 1964. Harold Wilson established good relations with Dublin; one of his first decisions was to return the remains of Sir Roger Casement, executed for his role in the 1916 Rising, for burial in Ireland. Economic links were strengthened by the signing of the Anglo-Irish Free Trade Agreement in December 1965, and a common desire to enter the Common Market enhanced this working arrangement. By 1967 it could be written: '...Harold Wilson now appeals more to the Dublin Government than any other British Prime Minister since the Treaty.'[14]

Such sympathy inevitably raised Unionist suspicions. They had much to be suspicious about. The Labour party had a tiny majority in the Commons and resented the influence of twelve Unionists voting with the Opposition on matters peculiar to the 'mainland'. Some of them formed the Campaign for Democracy in Ulster (CDU) in February 1965. They were joined after the 1966 General Election by Gerry Fitt, the new Republican Labour MP for West Belfast and – according to the *Belfast Telegraph* – 'one of the most effective non-Unionists who have been sent to Westminster by Northern Ireland'. By April 1967 the CDU was reporting 'how near the surface violence lies in current political life' in Ulster. Meanwhile Capt. O'Neill was enjoying what he has described as 'a working relationship' with Harold Wilson. Both men favoured reform.

Ancient quarrels

> To the Irish all History is Applied History and the past is simply a convenient quarry which provides ammunition to use against enemies in the present. They have little interest in it for its own sake. So when we say that the Irish are too much influenced by the past, we really mean that they are too much influenced by Irish history, which is a different matter.[15]

The unemployment marches of 1961 and 1962 gave way to the ritual commemorations which so flourish in Irish society. The 1960s provided enough anniversaries to tire even the most fervid marcher. 1962 saw the Jubilee of the signing of the Ulster Covenant when more than 400,000 had pledged themselves to resist Home Rule – hence a return to the spiritual wellspring of modern Ulster. 'Nonsectarian' Republicanism celebrated in 1963 the bicentenary of Wolfe Tone's death: the secular saint of the Republican movement allowed them to bask yet again in their own nonsectarian myths. 1966 proved a watershed. The Loyalists remembered the 5,500 of the 36th (Ulster) Division who died at the Battle of the Somme; and Republicans celebrated the 1916 uprising and the firing squads which followed. Both wallowed in memories of the blood sacrifice. Other commemorations followed (the centenary of the Fenian rising in 1967, and the centenary of James Connolly's birth in 1968), but by then the die was cast.

Now these were not simple folk celebrations. They represented heritages of bloody victory and bloody defeat; and they sat uneasily beside O'Neill's efforts to modernise. They were vital reminders of primordial passions, a quarry to be mined by political and spiritual zealots. To appreciate their significance we can contrast them with O'Neill's bid to establish 'secular Unionism'.

'Improving community relations was a major means by which Terence O'Neill sought full legitimation of his regime.'[16] The Prime Minister believed in the politics of the flamboyant gesture. He visited a Catholic secondary school in April 1964, an act 'historic' in an Ulster context. Shortly afterwards he granted recognition to the Northern Ireland Committee of the Irish Congress of Trade Unions, a body with headquarters in Dublin and therefore 'alien'. This he considered to be 'one of the most difficult hurdles' he surmounted. However his most spectacular production was his meeting with Sean Lemass at Stormont on 14 January 1965, the first occasion since partition on which the Prime Minister of the Republic was officially invited to Belfast. It was a meeting charged with great historical import and had been arranged without the knowledge of his Cabinet colleagues.

O'Neill judged it an outstanding success endorsed by the people at the General Election in November. Certainly it took his opponents by surprise. The Nationalist party hurriedly consulted with the Dublin authorities before accepting the role of official Opposition for the first time in their history. The worrying threat of the NILP to Unionism was diminished at the election when they lost two of their four Belfast seats. O'Neill's modernisation and community relations efforts had induced many 'liberals' to vote for the Unionist party for the first time. Full legitimation of his regime appeared a possibility, if only he could hold the Unionist umbrella together. He failed, and that failure probably began with the Lemass meeting. His ministerial colleagues feigned a sense of hurt and betrayal through his lack of consultation. They welcomed the meeting of course. They considered Lemass 'a moderate man with whom we should have been able to strike up a mutually useful relationship'. But there was this matter of trust. Faulkner thought that it was this unexpected meeting that 'started the slide away of support for O'Neill within the Unionist community', especially when Terence had the gall to represent 'all his critics as shell-backed reactionaries'.[17]

One man had no objection to being called a shell-backed reactionary, nor did he consider it expedient to couch his criticism in terms of wounded pride. Ian Paisley had not been born 'with silver spoons in gob'. His was the voice of authentic Ulster: 'The Ulster accent, a bastard lowland Scots, is harsh, and is given a sort of comic bluster by the glottal stop imported from Glasgow.'[18] The clamorous chant of 'O'Neill must go' increased in intensity after 1965. He would put a stop to O'Neill's bridge-building efforts: 'What do a bridge and a traitor have in common? Both cross to the other side.' Paisley was full of these simple Ulster aphorisms. They made great sense to a confused flock in an era of spiritual and political uncertainty. Paisley was 'his own man', an important quality in a face-to-face society. He was prepared to put his principles to the test (or 'nail his colours to the mast' as he constantly reminded his audience/congregation). Had he not been prepared to go to jail in 1959 after he exposed the apostate Methodist, Dr Donald Soper, by throwing a bible at him in Ballymena? He did, in fact, serve a three-month sentence in 1966 after he refused to sign a pledge of good behaviour. His fundamentalism was based on fighting ecumenism and modernism within the Reformed communion. His crusade had led him in 1966 to protest against a visit by the Archbishop of Canterbury to the Pope.

Yet he must not be seen as a theological Don Quixote if only because his theology cannot be separated from his politics. On occasion his political activity might suggest the village idiot – when Jack Lynch visited Stormont in December 1965, Paisley was photographed throwing snowballs at the Republic's Premier. But that would be to miss the point. The biblical analogy of David and Goliath is more appropriate. The snowballs did not have the power of the sling, and they may not even have had direction. Nonetheless Paisley had the arm and power of David; his arm was the destruction of O'Neill, and his overt strength was the Ulster Constitution Defence Committee and the Ulster Protestant Volunteers. The UCDC, formed in April 1964, had an uncompromising constitution. Article 17 read (in part): 'When the authorities act contrary to the Constitution (of Northern Ireland) the body will take whatever steps it thinks fit to expose such unconstitutional acts.' 'Whatever steps' meant precisely that.

He was conscious, too, of his role as Moderator of the Free Presbyterian Church. The religio-political connection was shown in June 1966 when he organised a protest against the policies of the Presbyterian Assembly. His march to the Assembly took him through Republican territory and a large-scale riot in which four policemen were badly injured. 'None of the marchers were hurt.

"When one thinks of over 600 people walking through such an onslaught unharmed," commented Paisley later, "one can only praise the Lord".'[19] A confrontation outside the Assembly headquarters led to the (later) resignation of the Governor of Northern Ireland following abuse heaped on his wife by the protestors, a humiliating public apology to the Assembly from the Minister of Home Affairs, and three months imprisonment for Paisley.

Political martyrdom suited Paisley. He was in competition with O'Neill for the 'soul' of Unionism, so, in that respect, an antipathetic style was important. The Prime Minister's genteel reminders to Loyalists to 'love thy neighbour' bore little fruit. Richard Rose found that 52 per cent of the population endorsed the use of violence to keep Northern Ireland protestant: 'The reasons given are few, simple and unambiguous: defence of Protestantism and the British connection, and opposition to Catholicism and the Republic.' Given the uncertainty about the constitution after the O'Neill-Lemass, meeting Rose's conclusion about Paisleyism is not altogether surprising: 'Defining Paisleyism at its broadest – at all costs to endeavour to keep Northern Ireland Protestant – would classify slightly more than half the Protestants in the Province as Paisleyites.'[20]

In fact Paisleyism was about more than the constitution and Protestantism:

> Political Paisleyism was proletarian, but religious Paisleyism attracted lower middle-class congregations which crammed the ample car park with their Cortinas. 'Do film the cars driving in,' a television crew was told by Mr Gunning, the chief secretary. 'It will show that we're getting a better class of person.'[21]

This inter-class support can be explained by reverting to O'Neill's modernism. The Matthew Plan had urged that a Belfast urban motorway system be constructed at the earliest possible moment. Unfortunately such a scheme would upset a settled way of living: '. . . going ahead with the motorway entailed the loss of land that could have been used to house over 4,000 families close to the city centre. This was at a time when the waiting list for houses had 9,000 families on it. A related cost . . . was the breakage of communities.'

Small traders would also be affected. Weiner had itemised the entry of large retail and distributive trades in Belfast since 1965, and quotes from the Belfast Urban Area Plan: 'As the trend to larger units and rationalisation of shopping in Redevelopment Areas takes effect, the number of shops will be reduced.'[22] For these people modernisation meant deprivation and uncertainty.

That uncertainty can be detected in attitudes on the Shankill Road during the 1960s. Frank Wright has sketched the demise of the NILP in the Woodvale constituency (which it held between 1958–65) and the rise of Paisley's Protestant Unionist Party in the local government elections of 1970:

> The major difference was that whereas in the former case the tacit assumption was that the interests of Protestant and Catholic workers were the same with regard to unemployment: in the latter case the Protestant unionist manifesto dwelt upon the preferential treatment which it was alleged that the Catholic working class on the Falls were receiving.[23]

The most dramatic manifestation of Protestant discontent occurred in June 1966 when the re-formed Ulster Volunteer Force (UVF) shot dead a young Catholic outside a pub on the Shankill area. The UVF claimed that the victims were members of the IRA and hence deserving of assassination; in fact they were innocent Catholics. In some Loyalist minds that distinction did not exist – all Catholics were Republicans and all Republicans deserved to be shot. O'Neill promptly used the Special Powers Act to proscribe the UVF. The last thing he needed was a shoot-out between Loyalist and Republican paramilitaries. By this stage it was clear that he had too many other problems on his mind.

The reform of local government

> If the Protestant State had been as homogeneously Protestant as the Catholic State was Catholic, then the Lemass-O'Neill *rapprochement* – followed up as it was by various 'official level' contacts – might indeed have given the results hoped for: the burying of old animosities, the adoption of a modern, pragmatic, developmental approach: better business, tourists, a pleasanter 'image' for all concerned.
>
> As it was it wasn't *just* a question of 'North-South relations'. There was the much more intractable question of the internal equilibrium between the communities inside Northern Ireland.[24]

Probably the most controversial recommendation in the Matthew Plan was the suggested creation of a Ministry of Planning and Development which was to subsume local government planning authority. Originally the idea was turned down by the Cabinet and was implemented only after O'Neill reshuffled the Cabinet and created the new Ministry when most of his colleagues were on holiday. So the creation of the Ministry of Development was yet another O'Neillite sleight of hand. His appointment of William Craig as his first Minister was an astute move since it tied the powerful Craig to the concept of development and allowed him to use his strong grass-roots support to 'sell' planning to the party activists.

The Ministry of Development was never too popular. It represented interventionist government treading in sensitive areas. The most sensitive was local government; for example, Stormont had never enjoyed a happy working relationship with Belfast councillors. One civil servant reports 'endless trouble' and 'constant disputes' between both bodies. City Hall resented interference from a 'parvenu Parliament and Government dating only from 1921', whereas it could trace its origins to the seventeenth century. 'They resented even more any attempts to equate them with other local authorities . . . Their deputations were testy with Ministers when not actively hostile.'[25]

Stormont seemed unmindful of City Hall pretensions as it undertook a campaign to modernise local government beginning in March 1966. It wanted to create a simplified, single-tier, strong local government system with a wide range of powers based on 12 to 18 'area councils'. Two White Papers advocating this philosophy were published in December 1967 (Cmnd 517) and July 1969 (Cmnd 530). They were strongly opposed by local interests. The Fermanagh Unionist Association, for example, produced what on the surface appeared to be a reasoned and 'modernising' objection when it argued that the plans were more akin to the age of the horse and cart because they sacrificed economy to satisfy 'local pride, local feeling and historical association'. It suggested instead three to five strong local government units. Fermanagh Unionists, however, were not the people to debate the merits of efficiency as opposed to local democracy. Their own record was a poor one. Their true philosophy of local democracy was summed up at a meeting in Enniskillen in February 1949 when the sitting Unionist MP warned that there was a Nationalist majority in the county:

We must ultimately reduce and liquidate that majority. This county, I think it can safely be said, is a Unionist county. The atmosphere is Unionist. The Boards and properties are nearly all controlled by Unionists. But there is still this millstone around our necks.[26]

Their objections were overruled not because there was no intrinsic merit in their case nor because some Cabinet ministers did not share their desire to keep local government – 'atmosphere' and all – Unionist, but because law and order was breaking down by 1969 and 'big brother' at Westminster was overseeing Stormont policy making. Thus the Northern Ireland Government proceeded on the basis that the province was to be treated as an English shire. It appointed a highpowered Review Body, the Macrory Committee, in December 1969 to recommend widespread changes in the local government system. The Committee's Report (Cmnd 546), published in May 1970, suggested the creation of 26 district councils with responsibility for such things as community facilities and environmental health. Essential services such as planning and education were to revert to central government departments. Reorganisation took effect on 1 October 1973 when the Ministry of Development became the planning authority for the whole of the province.

Macrory was Northern Ireland's Maud: 'The reorganisation was on a more radical scale than in England or Scotland and preceded them in time. Macrory stamped his imprint as indelibly on the administrative scene as, ten years earlier, Matthew had done on the physical.'[27] Unfortunately, Northern Ireland wasn't governed by the administrator's dream of efficiency. More mundane considerations reigned, the most important of which was the control of the local authorities. Government apologists for Macrory received a rough ride. Brian Faulkner stalked the province trying to sell the proposals: '. . . a large proportion of the audience was hostile in varying degrees. Many were local councillors who felt that their years of service to the community were being shabbily rewarded, others were suspicious and hostile to change'.[28] Faulkner glosses over the scale of hostility – the sense of loss was profound. O'Neillism had engendered an administrative revolution and, in the process, had denuded traditional Unionism of much of its power. It only remained for the Trojan horse of the civil rights campaign to complete that process.

Civil rights

It is frightfully hard to explain to Protestants that if you give Roman Catholics a good job and a good house, they will live like Protestants, because they will see neighbours with cars and television sets.

They will refuse to have 18 children, but if a Roman Catholic is jobless, and lives in a most ghastly hovel, he will rear 18 children on National Assistance.

If you treat Roman Catholics with due consideration and kindness, they will live like Protestants in spite of the authoritative nature of their Church.[29]

Throughout his autobiography a sense of personal hurt and a note of exasperation crops up when O'Neill examines his reaction to the civil rights movement. He could only have succeeded if Catholics had been prepared to anaesthetise their attitudes and aspirations for the duration of his premiership while he set about 'educating' the Protestant mind. However his patronising efforts did not encourage acquiescence from either community. He operated as if feudalism remained a feature of Western life, and he seemed to forget that inherent structural faults cannot be removed at a stroke. In short, he raised expectations which he was not in a position to fulfill.

Catholics in the professions were the first to note that their expectations were not being met; and they had some support from unexpected circles. The establishment-minded *Roundtable*, for example, commented in March 1964 that it 'is indicative of Government reluctance to admit that grievances exist and to forestall political attack that the National Assistance Board, the Housing Trust and the newly appointed Lockwood Committee on university expansion are without Catholic members'. A more damaging report appeared in *The Times* in April 1967, raising awkward questions about the rate of reform undertaken by the Prime Minister. O'Neill reacted angrily, but there is little doubt that that report had a wounding effect. Even towards the close of O'Neill's premiership in 1969 a survey of 22 public boards conducted by the Campaign for Social Justice (CSJ) demonstrated that the average level of Catholic membership on these boards had reached only 15 per cent.

Catholic grievances concerned unemployment, poor housing and electoral discrepancies. O'Neill's modernisation centred on the industrial infrastructure east of the Bann, at least until 1966: 'Of the remaining 7,000 (new jobs promoted under him), 2,000 were promoted in Derry City and Co. Derry in 1966 in a rather delayed start. In 1968–69, the distribution is much improved, but by that time the political and anti-O'Neill pressures had done their work.'[30] The debilitating effects of unemployment were most obvious in Derry City. There, in February 1967, it stood at an astronomical 20.1 per cent, when the British average was only 2.6 per cent, and Northern Ireland's was 8.1 per cent.

Derry people were not impressed by O'Neill's modernism. They felt isolated. They had lost their rail link with Donegal in 1953, with Dublin in 1965, and now the government was proposing to close the two lines to Belfast. (A compromise was reached and one single-track line was reprieved.) This sense of abandonment was compounded by the recommendation of the Lockwood Committee to construct a second university in Coleraine, a small town with no record of higher education, rather than Derry with its established Magee University College and a population viable enough to meet the needs of a university community. Besides these short-term complaints there were deep-rooted social and historical factors which made the Derry issue an unusually difficult one to solve. The geographer Alan Robinson considers that 'high fertility is the most significant demographic feature in Derry'. During this period 58 per cent of the population of Derry supported 42 per cent either too young or too old to be gainfully employed. Robinson believed that this made it more typical of tropical under-developed countries than of Western Europe, and that its age structure in 1961 was comparable to that of England and Wales in the mid-nineteenth century. The result was 'high youth dependency, overcrowded living conditions, low standard of living, high unemployment and migration'. Additionally, since high fertility affected the Catholic community more than the Protestant, it encouraged segregation.[31]

Historically Derry is vital in Unionist mythology. For the Loyalist the city is Londonderry, an area planted and maintained by the London companies in the early seventeenth century, Ulster's 'Maiden City' – so called because she was 'wooed but never won' by the Jacobite army in the siege of 1689. It is therefore, says Stewart, 'chiefly interesting because it provides the paradigm for the entire history of the siege of the plantation . . . it is enshrined in Protestant tradition ... as a set of historical tableaux ... depicting with vivid symbolism the courageous resistance of the Protestant settlement'.[32] For Catholics Derry derives its significance from the fifth-century monastic settlement of St Columba. The sexual symbolism of the 'Maiden City' is lost on them not because they are notably pietistic but because they recognise rape when they are the victims, and they believed themselves to be the victims of the longest rape in history, beginning in 1605. Hence Derry or Londonderry has a fascinating symbolic significance, a virtuous Protestant maiden, or a bedraggled Catholic wench.

The slogans of the 1960s centred on bad housing and high unemployment. The Government maintained that it was doing something about the latter. Housing was a different matter; it was the concern of local government. The Cameron Commission has examined Derry Corporation's electoral boundaries and housing policy; in Londonderry County Borough there was the following extraordinary situation in 1967:

	Catholic voters	Other voters	Seats
North Ward	2,530	3,946	8 Unionists
Waterside Ward	1,852	3,697	4 Unionists
South Ward	10,047	1,138	8 Non-Unionists
Total:	14,429	8,781	20

This inequitable ward distribution had been established in 1936, and was a vivid example of gerrymandering. It worked so long as there was no redistribution. However a problem arose when the Corporation ran out of land in the Catholic South Ward. Electorally, it could not afford to house Catholics in the remaining wards, nor could it contemplate extending the city boundaries since that might require an examination of the ward boundaries. Its solution was to do nothing; it stopped building homes.[33] The opposition retorted by raising awkward questions about the method of voting in local government elections.

Under the Elections and Franchise Act (N.I.) 1946, Ulster operated the ratepayer's franchise. Working on the principle of 'he who pays the piper calls the tune' only ratepayers had the vote – in some cases six votes depending on the rateable value of their business property. This scheme deviated from British practice after 1946, and when a NILP delegation complained to Chuter Ede, the Home Secretary, he hid behind the convention of referring the matter to the Northern Ireland Government. The entire Stormont opposition decided to fight for the principle of 'one man one vote' but could not prevent the passage of the legislation. In practice the ratepayer's franchise didn't make a crucial difference to local government control. In 1967 there were 694,483 registered local government electors and 973,724 Stormont electors. Budge and O'Leary examined its effect on Belfast County Borough during the 1960s and concluded that there was a bias, but that 'bias is so unsystematic as not to be the result of any concerted plan'.[34]

The bias was systematic in areas like Londonderry County Borough. And that, as Conor Cruise O'Brien succinctly put it, was another matter: 'Northern Ireland lives a siege: the image of besieged Derry, with the promise of its deliverance, is a far more poignant symbol for it than the wilted glory of the Boyne'.[35] Local politics in Derry was the soft underbelly of traditional Unionism. It could not accept the notion of a disloyal majority in control. I remember being told by a (Unionist) mayor of a Co. Armagh town with a substantial Catholic minority that 'Roman Catholics in Londonderry were different,' the 'difference' being explained by something in the air or its proximity to the border. Whatever the reason, they were not like *his* Roman Catholics. He offered a simple solution to quelling Catholic unrest in Derry – put the flamethrowers on them.

Loyalism was full of simple solutions. When the Civil Rights movement began agitating for British standards, loyalists concluded that it was a Republican/Bolshevist plot. That was easily handled – repression. A brief examination of the 'one man, one vote' issue illustrates that the campaign had a broad popular base, and that more than 'simple solutions' were called for.

A Lancaster Peace Research Centre observer commented in July 1966 that Catholics were being more assertive within the political system. Some had tried to reform the Nationalist Party in 1959 when they established a pressure group called National Unity. Failure to secure Nationalist compliance led to the formation of the National Democratic Party (NDP) in late 1964. The NDP held only one Stormont seat and its support was confined to Catholic areas in Belfast. Yet it was significant because its founders represented a generation of young Catholic graduates who believed that Irish unification could come about only through the consent of a majority in Northern Ireland; in other words the onus was on Nationalists to woo substantial Unionist support to the idea of a united Ireland.

Another pressure group, the Campaign for Social Justice in Northern Ireland (CSJ), was formed in Dungannon in January 1964, 'for the purpose of bringing the light of publicity to bear on the discrimination which exists in our community against' Catholics. Significantly its founders were 'respectable' members of the Catholic professional class, its leading light was a country doctor's wife. It concentrated on propaganda directed at British politicians. A more contentious organisation was the Northern Ireland Civil Rights Association (NICRA) founded in February 1967, preaching a policy of non-violent direct action and fighting for the more pressing social problems like housing and unemployment rather than issues of personal liberty. Both received assistance from the Stormont opposition. NILP had proposed a private member's Bill to outlaw religious discrimination in 1964, and had moved a resolution demanding reform of the local government franchise in May 1967. Both met predictable defeats. Henceforward political action switched to the streets.

1968 was a momentous year. It saw the death of Che Guevara in Bolivia; the extinction of Dubcek and the reformers in Czechoslovakia; widespread student rioting in Italy, Spain, France, West Germany, Mexico and the United States; and a fundamental challenge to the Unionist system in Northern Ireland. In February a NICRA press conference in London announced a more open challenge to Stormont's record on housing discrimination. In June Austin Currie, a young Nationalist MP, illegally occupied a council house in the Co. Tyrone village of Caledon. The house had been allocated to a nineteen year old unmarried Protestant girl, and Currie was able to use the widespread publicity he received to compare that allocation with the miserable housing conditions of many of his Catholic constituents. In August the first of a long line of civil rights marches was staged, this over a six-mile route in Co. Tyrone. Publicity again was valuable and whetted the appetite for further marches.

The next site chosen for demonstration was Derry on 5 October. NICRA saw it as the *locus classicus* of Unionist injustice and the more traditional loyalist held it to be a kind of holy city – if it had withstood the siege in 1689 it was not going to be breached for spurious reasons in 1968. The Government decided to take action, and the Minister of Home Affairs, William Craig, banned part of the route of the march. He reasoned that it would encroach on traditional Protestant territory – certainly Catholics had avoided parts of the route in the past. And he claimed that the march would clash with a traditional Orange demonstration which had been arranged for that day. In fact the latter had been arranged hastily as a device to be used against NICRA plans. In any event the march went ahead over the original route. The RUC threw up a cordon and a riot ensued. Seventy-seven civilians and eleven policemen were injured as rioting spread over into the Catholic west side of the city and continued throughout the night.

Events after 5 October followed an inexorable pattern. Here we shall pause to reflect on the impact of the early Civil Rights movement. It appears to have been motivated by a strong sense of moral outrage; it knew it had justice on its side particularly west of the Bann. The Cameron Commission agreed that the electoral arrangements were weighted against non-Unionists in Derry city, Armagh city, Omagh town, Co. Fermanagh and Dungannon Urban and Rural District Council. Housing policy has also 'been distorted for political ends in the Unionist-controlled areas to which we specifically refer (Derry, Omagh, and Dungannon). In each, houses have been built and allocated in such a way that they will not disturb the political balance' (para. 139). In his memoirs Capt. O'Neill accepts these criticisms: 'Any liberal-minded person must admit that the Civil Rights movements brought about reforms which would otherwise have taken years to wring from a reluctant Government.'[36]

Secondly, the slogans adopted by NICRA contributed to its initial success. Brian Faulkner rightly stresses its significance:

It sounded, to a world attuned to such protests, a positive humanitarian cry from an oppressed people. It also seemed to involve a very basic right . . . Many well-meaning but ill-informed people, even in Britain, were under the impression that the 'evil Unionist government' had made it illegal for Catholics to vote in elections.[37]

The Civil Rights Movement won the propaganda battle. Unionist ranks were divided and hesitant; often they reacted with truculence and inflexibility. Their working-class supporters bitterly resented being identified as part of the 'Protestant ascendancy': 'I think what especially angered poor Protestants was *precisely* that he (O'Neill) left them in slum houses while appearing to give Catholics the new goodies of life at their expense.'[38]

Another consequence concerned police reaction in Derry on 5 October (and later). The Cameron Commission (para. 229:14) alleged that police conduct on that day 'was in certain material respects ill-co-ordinated and inept. There was use of unnecessary and ill-controlled force in the dispersal of the demonstrators, only a minority of whom acted in a disorderly and violent manner'. Later demonstrations raised further complaints of police partiality; ultimately it centred on the issue of whether the Government was able to maintain 'peace, order and good government' evenhandedly. Catholic confidence in the police had never been very strong but after October 1968 it all but collapsed leaving a vacuum to be filled by unofficial 'law-enforcement' authorities.

Finally we must mention the degree of Republican infiltration into the Civil Rights movement. On 6 October the Minister of Home Affairs claimed that well-known Republicans had been seen on the Derry march. Cameron (para. 214) concurred: '. . . there is evidence that members of the IRA are active in the organisation, there is no sign that they are in any sense dominant or in a position to control or direct policy of the Civil Rights Association.' In fact the only Republican representative on the first Executive of NICRA was Kevin Agnew, a solicitor. The Commanding Officer of the Belfast IRA had declined nomination since his presence might embarrass NICRA. Since 1963 Republicans, disillusioned by the failure and futility of previous campaigns of violence, had embarked on a new strategy. They favoured a civil rights campaign as part of their strategy of 'revolution by stages', the first being to 'democratise' Northern Ireland: 'And because reforming Northern Ireland was such a crucial step, one which might never be completed if the 'Loyalist' population was unduly aroused, the Republicans were determined that all civil rights agitation be peaceful'.[39]

That strand of Republicanism which believed in the efficacy of non-violent direct action was in control until the Belfast riots in August 1969. Thereafter it had to compete with what became known as the Provisional IRA, much more traditional, more conservative, more 'Irish' and more inflexible. These two strands enable us to understand the contradiction in the civil rights campaign:

> ... when Northern Irish Catholic spokesmen demanded full British rights in 1968–69, they were not really, as they seemed to be, looking for assimilation into the British community; what they were really doing was more tactical: it was to turn the Ulster Protestant claim, 'Ulster is British,' into a weapon against the internal realities of the Ulster Protestant state. Only four years later the right claimed by the same spokesman was opposite in form: that of integration into a united Ireland.[40]

Conclusion

Over the past decade a community myth has arisen that Northern Ireland was 'a grand wee place' to live in before 1968. Everyone was prosperous and happy. Given the barbarity of the present campaign of violence there is much in this view that is attractive. But it does not square up to reality. Social conditions for many people in both communities were unbelievably harsh by British standards. Electoral and political irregularities did exist and contributed directly to the general misery. Northern Ireland was a 'scarcity society'. Only a massive injection of investment and good will could offer the blessings of a solution. Neither were available. In their place conspiracy theories arose. Fundamental Protestantism saw the hand of Moscow and the Vatican at work in every riot. Ulster had become the bastion of Protestantism in the Western World. Violent Republicanism failed to detect the strains in Unionism. It wrapped itself in the myth of the 'age-old struggle of the Irish people to be free', without explaining who precisely the 'Irish people' were.

The reality was more complex and more disheartening. In attempting to operate the Westminster model – rather than its peculiar Ulster version – O'Neill exposed the structural flaws. In his own Anglo-Irish fashion, with his sense of 'decency' and 'service', he set out to redress genuine grievances. But his brand of Toryism had little support in twentieth-century Ulster. A conception of politics as 'the conciliation of divergent interests' had never taken root in Northern Ireland. It was much more simple to settle conflicting claims by traditional methods. It was also much more deadly.

7 A State of Emergency

Generally speaking, the most perilous moment for a bad government occurs when it seeks to mend its ways. Only consummate statecraft can enable a king to save his throne when after a long spell of oppressive rule he sets out to improve the lot of his subjects.

Alexis de Tocqueville

What does normal mean? Jesus Christ Himself couldn't stick it. He asked for the bitter cup to be taken away, and He had only three days to suffer. We've gone through it now for three years. There's pressure weighing on us like the lid on a boiling pot.

Bogside resident[1]

The test of a policy designed to create public order in the midst of internal war is not whether it conforms to conventional liberal assumptions, but whether it produces order.

Richard Rose[2]

A chronology of events 1968–1983

In 1978 Sir Kenneth Newman described policing in Ulster a decade earlier as a 'Chief Constable's dream', with only 8,000 indictable offences to deal with and a 60 per cent clean-up rate. Since the first Civil Rights demonstrations that crime rate has soared almost sixfold, the clean-up rate is down to 20 per cent, and the death toll arising from civil disturbances has passed the 2,000 mark. At the political level the authorisation since 1969 of seven successive sets of institutions – Unionist Government, direct rule with an appointed advisory council, devolved coalition government, temporary direct rule, a Constitutional Convention, temporary direct rule again, and James Prior's 'rolling devolution' initiative – have added to the sense of bewilderment and shock shared by the whole population.

This short section attempts to find a way through this maze to pinpoint the political and constitutional landmarks of this time. Chronologically the period can be divided up into the years from

October 1968 to March 1972, when direct rule was imposed by the British government, and the years after direct rule. The first period is highlighted by growing Catholic assertiveness, increasing Protestant mistrust and self-doubt, and dithering Whitehall involvement in vain search of a coherent Ulster policy.

Catholic confidence can be traced through the Civil Rights Movement (CRM), which won most of what it had demanded as well as breaking up the apparently monolithic Protestant and Unionist alliance. The CRM asserted non-violence by adopting Martin Luther King, rather than an Irish nationalist hero, as its mentor. Further, its demands for 'civil rights and social justice' were palpably 'British'. But it was the missing demand which caused so much consternation: none of their very impressive propaganda exercises mentioned Irish unity as the ultimate solution to the Ulster question.

The campaign demonstrated deep historical animosities within the Unionist camp between the 'fearful' and the 'confident' Protestants. As early as 22 November 1968, Capt. O'Neill conceded (helped by some firm pressure from London) the majority of Catholic demands when he announced the establishment of an ombudsman, the dissolution of Londonderry County Borough Council (to be replaced by a Government-appointed Commission), franchise reform at local government level, a review of the Special Powers Act, and a points system to ensure the equitable allocation of local authority housing. By 23 April 1969, he had persuaded his party, by a majority of 28 to 22 votes, to accept the principle of one man, one vote in local government elections. Meanwhile, he had sacked his Minister of Home Affairs, had faced a backbench revolt, had lost three senior Cabinet Ministers through resignation, and had called a general election in February 1969 to enable him to continue with a broader mandate. That mandate was not forthcoming.

O'Neill resigned at the end of April when it was clear that he could carry his party no further along the road of reform. His successor, Major James Chichester-Clark, a distant relative, stayed in office for only two years, during which time he came under more direct pressure from the British authorities as well as the Unionist 'fearful'. His premiership is marked by a growing concern with 'security' and 'law and order'.

One feature of civil rights marches had been the growth of loyalist counter-demonstrations and increasing confrontations. The most violent incident occurred at an isolated beauty spot, Burntollet Bridge on 4 January 1969. The People's Democracy, a radical student offshoot of the civil rights campaign which placed no trust in O'Neill's reforming efforts, was ambushed by a becudgelled loyalist mob as it came to the end of a four-day march from Belfast to Derry. The attack was co-ordinated and vicious and led to some serious injury, especially since the RUC gave the marchers little or no protection.

Loyalists reacted by assuming that the People's Democracy march was an exercise in Republican provocation. It had encroached on the unwritten law of territoriality – each side knows its own boundaries and does not step outside them. The uneasy alliance between moderate Catholics and liberal Protestants broke down after Burntollet, especially since some RUC men had run amok in Derry on 4 January and had attacked innocent passers-by and the Catholic residents of Bogside. In retaliation, the Bogside was sealed off, a 'people's militia' formed, and 'Free Derry' constituted. Derry's Catholic population seceded – albeit for only one week – from the Northern Ireland state.

Civil rights demonstrations were no longer innocent diversions; violence was likely. Until August the only destructive work occurred away from demonstrations when attempts were made to blow up electricity generators in April. Assumed to be the work of the IRA, it was discovered that anti-O'Neill Loyalists had been responsible. Ironically those explosions led to the first influx of British troops; the Ministry of Defence announced on 20 April that 550 troops would be dispatched to aid the civil authority but that they would not be used to quell demonstrations or maintain public order. At a much later date Loyalists were to discover that the Army's presence raised questions about Northern Ireland's constitutional status.

'The Troubles' began in earnest, predictably in Derry, in August 1969. RUC incursions into the Bogside in January and April 1969 had led to internal police inquiries which their own Chief Constable described as 'most unsatisfactory'. He was referring in particular to the Devenny inquiry set up to establish which police officers were responsible for the death of a middle-aged man following a beating he had received in his home in the Bogside in April. Failure to uncover the culprits led the Chief Constable to complain of a 'conspiracy of silence' within his own force, and led Bogsiders to the conviction that justice would not be secured under the regime.

The Apprentice Boys of Derry hold their annual celebration of the relief of (Protestant) Derry from the forces of (Catholic) James II every 12 August. In 1969 the city was very tense when the Government refused to call off the march. The inevitable riot ensued and the bitter feud between residents and police broke out once again. On this occasion the Bogside had drawn up contingency plans to draw the RUC away from the area by fomenting riots elsewhere across the province. One riot centre was Belfast's Falls Road, where the RUC station was attacked by a Catholic mob.

The police chose to see this as an IRA plot. One reporter describes the scene in Belfast:

> The RUC had by now convinced themselves that they faced something approaching a Catholic revolt. Fantastically, in Great Britain, (sic), their senior officers had permitted the calling out of armoured cars mounted with heavy machine guns. Many RUC men also had 9 mm Sterling sub-machine guns as personal weapons. There was the absolutely clear feeling among the police that they faced a direct threat . . . the police would loose off burst after burst of sub-machine gunfire at something – or nothing. And the armoured cars began to career the lengths of the Falls Road emptying belts of heavy calibre ammunition in the direction of any supposed threat.[3]

By Saturday 10 August the official death toll had risen to eight, the injured numbered many thousands and hundreds of homes were either destroyed or badly damaged.

It was the Catholic communities of the Falls and Ardoyne areas which bore the brunt of the attack in the most serious rioting since the 1920s. Intimidation added to their problems. Over the next four years between 30,000 and 60,000 people were forced to leave their homes in the Greater Belfast area in what the Community Relations Commission considered to be the largest enforced population movement in Europe since 1945.

The immediate consequences of the death and destruction was the appearance of British troops in the streets of Belfast and Derry who were at first welcomed by the Catholic population. August 1969 represented nemesis for the RUC. Overall responsibility for security was placed in the hands of Lt. Gen. Sir Ian Freeland, General Officer Commanding (GOC) Northern Ireland, and a Commission under Lord Hunt (Cmnd 535) was established to inquire into the structure of the RUC and 'B' Specials. Its Report in October disarmed the RUC and led to the disbandment of the 'B' Specials. The Government also announced that Lord Scarman would head a tribunal to enquire into the disturbances. His Tribunal's Report (Cmnd 566) made the interesting point that in 'a very real sense our inquiry was an investigation of police conduct' (para. 3:1), and that, while a 'general case of a partisan force co-operating with Protestant mobs to attack Catholic people is devoid of substance' (3:2), there were 'six occasions in the course of these disturbances when the police, by act or omission, were seriously at fault' (3:7).

August 1969 also represented the first faltering steps by Westminster to control the situation. British governments adopted the strategy of 'direct rule by proxy' until that proved barren in 1972. A joint Communiqué (Cmnd 4154) issued by Belfast and London after a meeting in Downing Street on 19 August unfolded the plan. Joint working parties of officials of the two Governments were established to examine the extent and pace of the proposed reforms. Two very senior civil servants – one of whom had been Private Secretary at No 10 from 1964 to 1966 and Ambassador to Denmark from 1966 to 1969 – were dispatched to Belfast to occupy rooms adjacent to the Prime Minister and Minister of Home Affairs to oversee British policy and to report directly to London. This created resentment among the indigenous Civil Service, and placed the hapless James Chichester-Clark in the role of surrogate Prime Minister. Additionally it placed the 'mainland' representatives in a unique position to familiarise themselves with administrative procedures and decision-making processes at Stormont should the moment ever arrive when direct rule would need to be imposed.

From the outset it was clear that Stormont's conception of the problem differed from that of Westminster's. The latter adopted what was contemptuously referred to as a 'softly softly' policy, trying to talk down the many Catholic barricades in Belfast and Derry rather than resort to force. Security chiefs, for a period, were seen to consort openly with known Republicans. When that did not have immediate effect the strategy changed to the more conventional one of the security response coinciding with a change of government at

Westminster in mid-1970. The new Conservative Home Secretary, Reginald Maudling, gave the security forces their head and let them move into the Catholic ghettoes to 'root out' the enemy.

The most spectacular instance of this occurred in July 1970 when the GOC sanctioned a 34-hour curfew of the Lower Falls area of Belfast. The action cost five civilian lives and 75 injuries and uncovered 208 weapons, 250 lbs (113 kg) of explosives, 21,000 rounds of ammunition and eight two-way radios – a small return when compared with the massive antagonism it created among the Catholic community. The Army top brass failed to appreciate the fears and frustrations of Catholics and ignored developing tension between squaddies and civilians. Indirectly, Army actions were to serve as a recruiting agent for the Provisional IRA which emerged early in 1970 from the Catholic ghettoes, initially as a defensive body.

Unionist politicians remained dissatisfied with the security response. All but the most moderate saw an elaborate Republican plot unfolding before them. Street rioting was becoming more frequent and more sophisticated. The death of the first soldier on the streets of Northern Ireland in February 1971 convinced them that the IRA had declared war. Chichester-Clark demanded an increase in the number of troops. When that was refused he resigned in March 1971. His successor, Brian Faulkner, was a more astute and articulate politician who did not allow himself to be so easily led by his London masters. In fact he persuaded them that a massive internment swoop on all known Republican activists would halt the troubles at a stroke.

Internment had been moderately successful as a security measure when it had been used in the past, in 1921–24, 1938–45 and 1956–62. It began on 9 August 1971 when over 300 men were arrested and lasted until 5 December 1975, by which time 2,158 'graduates' had passed through the internment camps. As a political and security exercise it 'was a disaster. It led to terrific resentment'.[4] It failed miserably to control the violence: of the 172 who died violently in 1971 only 28 were killed before internment was introduced. The bulk of IRA activists escaped the security swoop largely because RUC intelligence files were so out of date. Many of those arrested initially had not been involved in the current crisis and so the whole operation was seen by Catholics as yet another attack on their community.

Internment without trial was meant, too, to be an intelligence gathering exercise but soon allegations of torture began to appear. Britain was arraigned before the European Court of Human Rights at Strasbourg on a charge of torturing 14 men in army barracks in Northern Ireland between August and October 1971. The alleged techniques used included covering suspects' heads with black hoods for long periods, exposing them to continuous and monotonous noise of a kind calculated to make any communication impossible, making them stand against a wall with their legs apart and hands raised against the wall for continuous periods of six or seven hours at a time, and finally depriving them of food and sleep: 'The main techniques used . . . were designed, in plain terms, to send men out of their minds.'[5] The Irish Government brought charges against Britain before the European Court in 1971, but it was not until January 1978 that the Court finally found against Britain for degrading and inhuman treatment.

The whole episode was extremely embarrassing for Britain. By September 1976 she had settled compensation in the region of £10,000 to £12,000 for 12 of the original 14 victims. She had established her own enquiry under Lord Compton (Cmnd 4823, London, 1971) which concluded that the techniques constituted 'physical ill-treatment' but not brutality. The novelist Graham Greene's retort captures the right condemnatory note:

'Deep interrogation' – a bureaucratic phrase which takes the place of the simpler word 'torture' and is worthy of Orwell's *1984* – is on a different level of immorality than hysterical sadism or the indiscriminate bomb of urban guerrillas. It is something organised with imagination and a knowledge of psychology, calculated and cold blooded, and it is only half condemned by the Compton investigation.[6]

Furthermore no punishments had been meted out, and no promotions – army or police – had been affected by those guilty of using the technique.

The internment saga poisoned relations between the army and the Catholic community over four years, but one particular incident had

an immediate and catastrophic effect. It occurred in Derry on
Sunday 30 January 1972 when an illegal anti-internment march
resulted in the statutory skirmish between a youthful mob and some
army regiments. After allegations that shots had been fired on the
army from the Bogside, paratroopers moved in firing recklessly and
killed 14 male civilians. All of the victims were innocent in the sense
that the authorities felt it necessary to make out-of-court payments
to their relatives and an official tribunal consisting of Lord Widgery,
the Lord Chief Justice, (HL 101, HC 220, 1972) failed to prove that
any of the victims had been carrying weapons. 'Bloody Sunday' had
a profound effect on Ulster Catholics and on the Heath Government. The former totally and irrevocably withdrew their consent
from the Unionist regime, and the Conservatives reacted by
establishing the Widgery tribunal and holding urgent talks with
Brian Faulkner and his ministers. Those talks broke down on the
vital issue of which government would control security; consequently London invoked its sovereign powers under s.75 of the 1920
Act, prorogued Stormont and imposed direct rule.

   The imposition of direct rule had a traumatic effect on a people
grown used to untrammelled one-party government over half a
century. The imagery and the substance of power had disappeared
overnight, to be replaced by a Secretary of State for Northern
Ireland governing through three junior Ministers and an Advisory
Commission of eleven Ulster 'notables' appointed by Westminster.
Brian Faulkner reacted by moving toward extreme loyalist opinion.
He supported a two-day loyalist strike which paralysed industry in
most areas of Northern Ireland; and he told a mass rally at Stormont
that he and his Ministers not only understood their feelings but
shared them. These sentiments resembled de Gaulle's address to the
French *colons* in Algeria in 1958: 'Je vous ai compris . . .' – the
analogy is appropriate since de Gaulle went on to betray the colons
and, in the eyes of most loyalists, Faulkner did the same.

   He and his former colleagues acted as a sort of government-in-
exile, busily preparing for the day when it would be recalled to
power. Every opportunity was used to attack the administration,
especially on matters of law and order. His more moderate
colleagues found all of this hard to stomach and within six months
three former Cabinet Ministers had resigned because they could not
accept the extremism of the party. At the other end of the spectrum

loyalists reacted by forming the Ulster Defence Association (UDA), a para-military body risen from the Protestant ghettoes with the ostensible aim of defending its territory from IRA incursions. Its existence proved that the major restraint on Protestant violence was removed now that Stormont had been prorogued.

It was estimated that the UDA numbered 50,000 men within three months of its birth. The increasing use of industrial stoppages, of illegal marches by masked and uniformed Protestants, of sit-downs, of armed confrontations between the Army and UDA, and of barricading off Protestant areas illustrated the deterioration of relations between loyalists and the Secretary of State's office. With the rapid increase in 'motiveless murders' (to use the argot of the authorities) – 80 Catholics and 38 Protestants were murdered in the nine months following Britain's takeover – the regime had to act. It began interning loyalists early in 1973; they reacted by calling a one-day strike in February in which five people were killed.

Yet the lines between the Government and disaffected majority were kept open, largely through the efforts of the Secretary of State, William Whitelaw. He moved with much greater stealth than the Prime Minister, who had taken to lecturing Protestants on the obligations as well as the rights of membership in the United Kingdom (November 1972), and of reminding them that many on the mainland considered them to be 'disloyalists' (March 1973). Whitelaw was much more conciliatory. He pursued a policy of steady release of IRA internees – but not at such a rate as would offend Protestant opinion absolutely. As a *quid pro quo* he stressed the economic advantages of the Union; announcing in May 1972, for example a £35 million expansion plan for the ailing Belfast shipyards which would provide 4,000 extra jobs. All these efforts won him the (not entirely hostile) loyalist epithet of 'Willy Whitewash'.

With the rate of violence increasing it became imperative to seek out a political solution. (In 1972 145 members of the security forces were killed as compared to 59 the previous year.) Towards the middle of 1972 Britain moved into its most creative period in Ulster since the regime was established. A meeting with the Provisionals was arranged by Whitelaw in July 1972 in London during a 13-day ceasefire. It came to nothing – not surprisingly, since their *idée fixe* was the reconquest of Ireland, nothing more and, certainly, nothing less. It caused him some embarrassment when the Provisionals leaked information about the meeting, although it may have had the long-term advantage of forcing him to concentrate his energies on the elected politicians.

The first attempt to get all the parties around a conference table to discuss the future government of the province was a conference in Darlington in September 1972 attended by only three parties. A month later a Green Paper, which offered some comfort to both communities, was published. Northern Ireland's constitutional position was guaranteed so long as the majority desired it – hence the Border Poll of 8 March 1973 in which the Protestant electorate overwhelmingly endorsed the constitutional status quo, and Catholics overwhelmingly abstained. Anti-partitionists were granted an 'Irish dimension', a device to encourage dialogue and strengthen economic links between both parts of Ireland. The most radical suggestion concerned the creation of a 'power-sharing' (or coalition) government.

A White Paper – *Northern Ireland Constitutional Proposals* (Cmnd 5259) – followed on 20 March 1973, released with the minimum of publicity lest it stir up a loyalist backlash. It proposed the return to a devolved system of government centred around a unicameral Assembly of 78 members elected by the single transferable vote system. Sovereignty would remain at Westminster with a Secretary of State for Northern Ireland to oversee relations between Belfast and London; security matters would be Westminster's responsibility for the foreseeable future; the Special Powers Act would be repealed and replaced by those provisions absolutely necessary during an emergency and acceptable to Parliament. A Council of Ireland, first mooted in the 1920 Act, was to be reinstated, and power-sharing at executive level to be imposed:

> . . . it is the view of the Government that the Executive itself can no longer be solely based on any single party if that party draws its support and its elected representation from only one section of a divided community. The Executive must be composed of persons who are prepared to work together by peaceful means for the benefit of the whole community . . . (para. 52)

The Secretary of State was to have ultimate power in the selection of the Executive.

Elections for the Assembly were held on 28 June and negotiations to form a power-sharing government began almost immediately, culminating in the creation of an Executive-Designate on 22 November. Three parties – the SDLP, (the major representative of the Catholic community, with 19 seats in the Assembly), the Alliance Party (a biconfessional centre party holding 8 seats) and a majority of the Unionist Party led by Brian Faulkner (23 seats) – formed the Executive, which sat for the first time on 1 January 1974. The Assembly Opposition was composed of a melange of anti-Faulkner loyalists holding 27 seats. On three occasions their opposition was so obstructive that the police had to be called into the Assembly. Despite these interruptions 'power-sharing' seemed to be working satisfactorily, demonstrating that Catholic and Protestant could work in harmony at the highest level, and, just as important, that Catholic members of the Executive were both capable and loyal. Nevertheless the experiment had collapsed within five months, the victim of a 'strike' orchestrated by the UDA.

The Ulster Workers' Council (UWC) Strike of May 1974 – for so it was called – restored, temporarily at least, loyalist self-respect. They had demonstrated that their most powerful bargaining card was not violence but the withdrawal of their labour. Their strategy was masterly, turning off the wheels of industry – gas and electricity (with sewerage to follow, if necessary) – one at a time. They out-manoeuvred the Army, who saw the strike in terms of a day-to-day tactical exercise rather than as the fundamental challenge to the system which it was. They outbluffed Harold Wilson's despised Labour Government which had come into office in February, and they defeated the 'united Ireland' implications in the proposed Council of Ireland.

The strike succeeded largely because the Protestant people felt so politically frustrated. They believed that they had been kicked around since 1968 by 'civil righters' and perfidious Albion, and that they had been hoodwinked by one of their own leaders, Brian Faulkner, who had been ambivalent in his attitude toward the SDLP.[7]

They had demonstrated, therefore, their community strength through the exercise of their veto. But it was a negative power. The Provisional IRA had welcomed the strike if only because it tied down 17,500 troops and caused untold damage to the Ulster economy. They laid down their arms for the duration of the strike happy to rest away from the front line and happy in the knowledge that the implications of the power-sharing concept would not be realised. In particular they had feared the establishment of a common area of law enforcement throughout Ireland so that those guilty of 'political' crimes could be tried wherever they were found. They had benefited from the fact that the Republic's Constitution did not permit extradition from the Republic to the United Kingdom on political charges; between 1971 – September 1975 49 extradition warrants had been received in Dublin from the RUC, yet no-one had been extradited.

Within a few months Westminster made another attempt to bring the parties together again. In July it decided to establish a constitutional Convention 'to consider what provisions for the government of Northern Ireland would be likely to command the most widespread acceptance throughout the community'. The Convention was dominated by 47 anti-power-sharers, who were opposed by an amalgam of 31 members who were in favour of some form of partnership government. It met during the second half of 1975 but failed to reach agreement, despite some initial hope that a faction of the Unionists would be able to reach agreement with the SDLP. One outstanding feature of the Convention was its use of inter-party talks to bring about agreement. Despite this, the loyalists forced through a majority report on 7 November which called for a return to simple majority rule on the basis of a federal constitution. It was unacceptable to the British Government, which asked the parties to reconvene. This they did early in 1976 but yet again general agreement seemed elusive.

Perhaps the Convention's only real advantage was that it helped 'to dissipate Loyalist euphoria which was being swiftly translated into uncompromising demands for a return to the Stormont system of government'. It served, then, as a 'distraction' and acted as a 'buffer between the UWC strike and indefinite direct rule'.[8] And yet at one stage it held out some hope when William Craig, a respected (because hard-line) Loyalist leader, suggested an emergency coalition government on British war-time precedents which would have permitted the Catholic opposition to share in power. The suggestion was sabotaged by other Loyalists before it was given proper consideration by all the parties.

With the failure of the Convention British policy concentrated on the art of inertia. Merlyn Rees, who had presided over the collapse of the power-sharing executive and of the Convention, was replaced in September 1976 by Roy Mason as Secretary of State. Mason attempted to build his reputation on keeping the Ulster economy reasonably buoyant and pursuing a security policy which would reduce violence to an 'acceptable' level. Apart from striking a bargain with Unionists at Westminster to keep the minority Labour government in office, no real political initiative was undertaken. In return Northern Ireland was promised increased representation in the Commons and Mason's team exercised a calculated contempt towards local politicians operating without a representative forum.

Following the Conservative victory in May 1979 Humphrey Atkins, a man without previous Cabinet experience or any knowledge of Ulster, was appointed Secretary of State. Prodded on by prominent Irish-American politicians he published a discussion paper, 'The Government of Northern Ireland: A Working Paper for a Conference' (Cmnd 7763) in November. The conference met early in 1980 attended by the APNI, DUP and SDLP (the Official Unionists refused to participate). Another Paper, 'The Government of Northern Ireland: Proposals for Further Discussion' (Cmnd 7590), appeared in July. It narrowed the political options to another form of power-sharing or a system of majority rule with a minority blocking mechanism. Once again there was no common ground for an internal settlement. Meanwhile Mr Atkins was engrossed in the hunger strike. That single issue dominated 1981. By September he was moved to the Foreign Office, the hunger strike not resolved, and with no sign of political movement. He departed as he arrived . . . bewildered and bemused.

His successor, James Prior, brought with him a formidable reputation, a keen ambition and a high-powered team. He felt the need to make an impact on Northern Ireland affairs which would be felt beyond the province. So, in April 1982, he launched yet another blueprint, 'Northern Ireland: A Framework for Devolution' (Cmnd 8541) modelled on the Atkins options but more flexible and more gradual – 'rolling devolution'. It was ingenuous but attracted no warm enthusiasm. With some skill and tenacity Mr Prior pushed his scheme through Westminster. In Northern Ireland, however, he found it much more difficult to have it widely accepted.

The politics of the last atrocity

Christ, it's near time that some small leak was sprung

In the great dykes the Dutchman made
To dam the dangerous tide that followed Seamus
Yet for all this art and sedentary trade
I am incapable. The famous

Northern reticence, the tight gag of place
And times; yes, yes. Of the 'wee six' I sing

Where to be saved you only must save face
And whatever you say, you say nothing.

Smoke-signals are loud-mouthed compared with us.[9]

The dominant themes of the past 15 years have been death and destruction. It is difficult to convey to the outside observer the sense of futility, anger, bitterness which the present campaign evokes. Northern Ireland is a small landmass composed of tightly-knit communities. The demography of violence illustrates its containment within relatively few areas, in particular Belfast and Derry where, in the period 1969–75, 72 per cent of deaths, 91 per cent of injuries resulting from civil disorder, 55 per cent of bombing, 33 per cent of gun battles, and 83 per cent of armed raids took place. Rural violence has been concentrated in areas bordering the Irish Republic and the 'Murder Triangle' in Mid-Ulster.[10] In the same period Richard Rose has calculated that nearly one family in every six has had a father, a son, a nephew or an aunt killed or injured in the Troubles.[11] Moreover, British army search procedures subsequent to internment have resulted in up to 75,000 household searches per year in a society of some 400,000 households.

On the economic front, violence and the recession have taken a severe toll. Manufacturing industry now employs approximately 95,000 people, a decline of about 47 per cent since 1970. Unemployment rose from 36,000 in 1970 to 119,843 by October 1983. The province has become so unattractive that a 1983 MORI poll showed that Northern Ireland came 19th out of a list of 20 desirable investment locations in Western Europe. A consequence has been Government reliance on high-risk investment in areas of high unemployment; for example, £80–£90 million was poured into the ill-fated De Lorean sports-car project in west Belfast. These figures might have been worse and were off-set by the recruitment of some 7,000 civilian searchers to protect commercial and public buildings, by a heavy migration during the 1970s at a rate of over eight per thousand of the population, and by an expansion of the public sector from about 50 per cent of all employees in employment in 1970 to a figure of 65 per cent by 1980. Not surprisingly, the United Kingdom subvention to, or on behalf of, Northern Ireland increased from £74 million in 1969–70 to £1,177 million in 1982–83 (and that excluded £143 million for the British Army presence in Northern Ireland). Finally, a detailed analysis by the New Ireland Forum calculated that the Troubles had cost taxpayers in both islands about £6 billion, and that the economies had been affected adversely to the tune of £5 billion.[12]

The Protestant community. The Ulsterman did not react to the figures on violence as would a statistician. There was, and is, an ambivalence about it in both communities. After all, the Ulster Volunteer Force armed itself in the Home Rule crisis of 1912 to resist Ulster's incorporation in a Home Rule crisis; and the men of 1916 laid down the ultimate blood sacrifice in their centuries-old struggle for freedom.

To begin with, the Loyalist population in general displayed the most reticence about the use of force to achieve political ends; but even that statement needs to be qualified and explained. H. A. Lyons' analysis of arrested rioters for a two-year period beginning 2 May 1969 indicates that more Protestants (55 per cent) were arrested for their activity than Catholics,[13] but that this trend is reversed in the second year. These figures will not surprise insiders, especially those living in Belfast's Catholic ghettoes who welcomed the British army in 1969 as a protection for their community against incursions by the police and the Loyalists.

It is only when we look at it in a broader perspective that we can see the true nature of Protestant violence. The Loyalist activist operated under much greater constraints than did his Republican counterpart. His mission was an essentially conservative one – to preserve Ulster, its way of life and its bricks and mortar – which forbade, for the most part, the use of spectacular methods such as car bombs or the destruction of property. He also operated under the myth of the 'law-abiding Ulsterman' – it was they who upheld the constitution and a traditional way of life against the destructive force of Republicanism. Hence their development as a defensive people looking after the welfare of their own community. That mentality can be seen in the very name of the major Loyalist paramilitary group, the Ulster *Defence* Association.

If we examine the pattern of Loyalist violence we find very little evidence of clashes with the security forces. Ironically, the first policeman to die in the present troubles was killed on the Shankill Road in October 1969 after the publication of the Hunt Report – ironically, that is, in that he was killed by a Loyalist gunman protesting against the emasculation of the forces of law and order. One reason why the Army was reluctant to square up to Loyalists during the 1974 strike was that it did not see the Protestants as the enemy. No, their task initially was to defend their community.

Their leaders arose from a community ethos distrustful of their own political leadership who had allowed the argument to go by default, contemptuous of the civil rights pretensions to be 'British', fearful for their 'privileges' and their way of life, and bitterly angry at the failure to 'root out Republican gunmen'. Most had begun their political activity as vigilantes within their own neighbourhood. It gave them time to discuss the failure of Unionism and the quality of their own lives. Virtually all of them could recount some Republican atrocity given the fact that from mid-1971 the Provisional IRA launched a full-scale attack on the province's institutions, and, in many cases, its people. And they possessed that sensitive, selective folk memory of the oppressed 'minority' (in an all-Ireland context). Loyalist misdeeds were less spectacular than Republican ones; they specialised in sectarian assassinations. Their greatest victory, the dismantling of the power-sharing Executive after the UWC strike in May 1974, signalled their strength at the point of production rather than the local community. It reinforced the community myth. Despite massive intimidation at the beginning, what memory retained was a disciplined work force and community which had successfully organised itself against its own destruction.

It is in this context that we must understand the tenacity of the

Ulster Protestant and the righteousness of their path even when this entails an alliance with paramilitaries.

> They [the paramilitaries] are as representative of their community as any other more acceptable institution. If they represent a dark side to the nature of that community then it is because that side exists within the community and within the individuals who belong to it . . . Abstracting it from the context within which they occur and relating it to other presumed species of what is sometimes described as a world revolutionary movement, we ignore at our peril the particularity of their origin, and of their development, which in fact determines their existence.[14]

The Catholic community. To understand the relationship between the Catholic community and the IRA we need to adjust the focus to encompass both the immediate and the historical. The 'immediate' coincides with the Civil Rights campaign and the horror of August 1969. The Catholic folk memory allows that no Civil Rights were conceded without bitter struggle and fierce resistance by the Unionist government. The events of August 1969 demonstrated their vulnerability, particularly in the Belfast ghettoes, highlighted the extreme partiality of the RUC – a partiality which they believed had existed anyway from 1922 – and concentrated their minds on their own defence.

Catholics began the present campaign, then, with little respect for the official upholders of law and order, and 'Free Derry' and 'Free Belfast' convinced them of the need to look after their own interests. The police and, after a short honeymoon period, the Army were fair game. Eammon McCann has described a 'sudden generation of kamikaze children' being reared in the Bogside: 'The Saturday riots became a regular thing. It was known as 'the matinée . . . the hooligans were the sons and daughters of the area, and however much their activities may have been regretted or condemned there could be no question of any section of the people backing the army *against* them.'[15]

But this was no simple hooligan problem. It was much, much more literally a matter of life and death – and Catholics believed they had no-one to defend them. The wall slogan 'I.R.A. – I Ran Away' captures the bitterness felt by many ghetto dwellers for their erstwhile defenders in August. The entire IRA arsenal in Belfast at the time 'consisted of 22 guns of various makes and models'.[16] That is a fact of the greatest importance. We have seen that the Republican leadership had been concentrating on social revolution rather than armed struggle, but after August the Catholic community 'did not call for more oratory or marches, or appeals to a non-existent class solidarity . . . It called for guns to defend Catholic homes. The men who brought the guns and were able to use them would have the key to the situation in the Catholic ghettoes, and the initiative elsewhere.'[17]

After a period of intense internal debate within the movement, the Provisional IRA emerged in December 1969. It split from the 'Official' movement on ideological grounds and the question of the armed struggle. By January 1970, when the split became public knowledge, there were two IRAs and two Sinn Feins (the political wing of the armed movement). The adoption of the title 'Provisional' is significant because it is borrowed from the 1916 Proclamation of the 'Provisional Government of the Irish Republic'. Its identification with Ireland's dead heroes was important in the mythology of the movement. It established them in Catholic eyes as being the true heirs of the Republican tradition, and gave them:

> . . . three ready-made assets: an inspiring revolutionary tradition that granted legitimacy, authorised an army without banners, a demonstrably viable alternative to the institutionalised sectarian injustice of the Northern Ireland establishment in Tone's Republic, and an organisational core of trained and zealous men to direct any rebellion . . .[18]

They were not, then, akin to the 'urban guerrillas' who had sprung up throughout Western Europe in the late 1960s. The 'Provos' were much more part of 'the people', deeply rooted in the community, and possessing historical precedents which went back at least to the mid-nineteenth century.

We should remember that they were welcomed first and foremost as defenders of the Catholic ghettoes. In that respect they were a symptom, and not a cause, of the troubles. To begin with their activity was only on a small scale. (The *Sunday Times* Insight Team could record only two relatively minor shooting and bombing incidents in which the Provos were involved by mid-1970.) 'At the beginning of 1970, there were not more than a few hundred Provos and their overwhelming concern was with the acquisition of arms in order to defend the Catholics of the North. No one was opposed to the presence of the British Army, rather the contrary but no one wanted to be caught defenceless again.[19]

Officially the 'war' began on 7 February 1971 when Major Chichester-Clark announced that Northern Ireland was at war with the Provisionals following the killing of the first British soldier in the province the previous day. By that stage the IRA was well prepared for the struggle, as the statistics below suggest.[20] 1972 was the most horrendous year for deaths through violence; after 1976 a diminishing pattern is established although 108 died violently in 1981, the year of the hunger strike.

| | *Yearly Figures for* | | | |
	1969	*1970*	*1971*	*1972*
Shootings	Not available	213	1,765	10,628
Explosions	Not available	153	1,022	1,382
Explosives used	Not available	746 lb (338 kg)	10,972 lb (4,977 kg)	47,462 lb (21,528 kg)
Explosives neutralised	Not available	59 lb (27 kg)	3,001 lb (1,361 kg)	19,978 lb (9,515 kg)
Deaths:				
RUC/RUCR	1	2	11	17
Army/UDR	Nil	Nil	48	129
Civilians	12	23	114	332

It would be a mistake, however, to assume that the terrorists are a spent force. Their campaign has been an object lesson in ingenuity and callousness. They have demonstrated considerable technological expertise in their use of explosives ranging from the crude but effective car bomb to more sophisticated incendiary bombs and those with anti-handling devices. Whether it has exploited the pretensions of liberal democracy and emergency legislation or concentrated on the spectacular assassination – Christopher Ewart-

Biggs, British Ambassador to Ireland (July 1976), Airey Neave, Conservative spokesman on Northern Ireland (April 1979), Lord Louis Mountbatten (August 1979), Sir Norman Stronge, former Speaker at Stormont, and his son James (January 1981), and Rev. Robert Bradford, Unionist MP for Belfast South (November 1981) – the terrorist propaganda machine has been of the highest order.

But we cannot explain continuing Provo survival (and that of the more reckless and vicious Irish National Liberation Army) solely on its military success and communications sophistication. Callousness and cynicism combined with Catholic ambivalence towards violence is a large part of the explanation. The New Ireland Forum analysis highlights the extent to which Catholics were the victims of their soi-distant republican protectors. Republicans have been responsible for the majority of the 2,300 deaths since 1969, and of the 1,297 civilian fatalities no less than 773 were Catholics. A similar picture emerges if we examine the major centres of violence and of its economic consequences – the Catholic working class has been the major victim. When the IRA did move on to the offensive, notably after the internment debacle in 1971, they imposed themselves on the Catholic community as protector and moral guide. Knee-cappings were a common punishment for 'deviants' – who tended to be defined in a narrow puritanical manner – after a summary trial. Those who passed on information to the security forces were sentenced to death. It was the Provisionals themselves rather than the community who decided who was a deviant and who was an informer. It is ironical that some of those who complained bitterly of Unionist 'kangaroo courts' and RUC 'rough justice' were not at all slow to resort to the same tactics.

And yet there is no evidence of wholesale abhorrence in the Catholic community of what is being done in their name by their self-appointed protectors. The most spectacular instance of Catholic ambivalence and of Provisional opportunism occurred during the 1981 hunger strike. To explain: for twelve years the Provisionals and the authorities were locked in battle over prison conditions – were convicted terrorists prisoners of war or criminals? They were granted special category status in 1972 by Mr Whitelaw in an attempt to woo them towards political discourse. He failed and had presented them with facilities to organise inside prison and a measure of respectability outside. His successor, Merlyn Rees, began phasing out special category from 1 March 1976. But that left two categories: those enjoying privileges until their release, and those jailed after March who were refused all concessions. The Provisionals exploited this anomaly. They refused to wear prison clothing and, after two years of stalemate, they began a 'dirty' protest by destroying cell furniture and failing to use the toilet facilities. By mid-1980 their morale was low and their supporters outside disillusioned. At that stage they made a last desperate bid through the hunger strike, a device which had already claimed twelve Republican victims in this century and which had a noble tradition in their mythology. The hunger strike produced some results, with an agreed settlement on prison clothing reached on 18 December 1980. However the agreement was breached when the prison authorities would not accept clothing brought in by prisoners' relatives.

A second and deadly phase began in March 1981; Bobby Sands, Provisional Officer Commanding in the Maze Prison, started a lone protest. If his strike ran its expected duration he would be dead by Easter, a festival potent with the imagery and symbolism of the spilled blood of the risen Christ. He was followed by volunteers at carefully chosen intervals and from a wide geographical spread to extract the maximum emotion. By September another nine strikers had followed Sands to his self-induced death, but not before he had become MP for Fermanagh/South Tyrone at an April by-election. 'Your vote can save this man's life' had the right emotive effect. His seat was retained in August by a Provisional Sinn Fein nominee, Owen Carron, and the political atmosphere had been polluted.

The hunger strike was a continuation of the IRA campaign by other means. The martyred bodies would serve as witness to the relentless fight for Ireland's freedom. Their self-image is one of a revolutionary vanguard and of the sacred keepers of the nation's history: 'we take our inspiration and our experience from the past', an inspiration, they contend, which extends back to Christ – 'Greater love hath no man than this, that a man lay down his life for his friends' occupied an essential place in hunger strike propaganda. It brought out in thousands a pietistic Catholic community, with a folk memory of the persecuted Church still fresh, to lend unwitting support to the IRA. In short, Provisional strategy was 'a carefully devised campaign to take possession of the entire tradition of Irish

Republicanism' by 'the primitive force of a symbolic act' and by breaking 'the relation between politics and discourse':

> The IRA can hardly hope to achieve its aim by force of argument, definition and reason. They must transcend the terms of any such discourse. The only way to do that is by taking some morally intimidating course of action, something that requires courage, passion and selflessness. Discourse can only be transcended by action: inside a prison, action can only take a symbolic form all the more potent for being irrational and in every respect exorbitant. There is no gesture more compelling than the hunger strike, and ideally the hunger strike till death.[21]

The strike petered out on 3 October with the intervention of the prisoners' relatives. The cost had been enormous. It revitalised the terrorists, stepped up violence, further polarised the communities, and reawakened Irish-American prejudices and generosity to the Republican cause. Fundamentally, it diminished the role of politics. Political leadership in London, Belfast and Dublin lacked the vision to arrive at compromise and could not match the seductive appeal of easy solutions to complex problems. This 'degenerate fondness of tricking shortcuts' made the politician redundant and moved the militant into the centre of the stage.

One victim was the SDLP, founded in 1970 to offer the Catholic community an alternative to violence. It was remarkably successful in building a powerful electoral base and in presenting an intellectually forceful case for anti-partitionism in adverse circumstances. Its presence in government in 1974, the first 'Catholic' party to do so, and the outstanding success of the party leader, John Hume, in easily winning a seat to the European Parliament direct elections in June 1979, gave Catholic politics a respectability and a visibility beyond the province. But the hunger strike challenged all that. SDLP refusal to nominate a candidate in the April by-election, and again in August, implied tacit support for the campaign. It was nothing of the sort. Simply it was an acknowledgement that this was ground where the Provisionals were too strong – better to fight another day when discourse would overcome intimidation – and it was a protest against Westminster's handling of the question. That was not how it was seen. Given that the party refused unconditional support to the security forces commentators referred again to the communal ambivalence towards violence.

The Peace People, founded in August 1976 after three children had been killed by an IRA car fleeing from the army, was another victim of such attitudes. In a curious sense the hunger strike had been a distorted image of the peace campaign. Both relied on moral fervour, revivalism on a grand scale, and both gained from superficial news media analyses. But there the comparisons end. The Peace People were patently nonsectarian; in fact their support across the community divide meant that they did not take firm root inside any one community and, in consequence, withered.

It is conceivable that some of those involved in the peace movement were motivated by the same Christian compassion to support the hunger strike. How do we explain this strange ambivalence shared by Irish people generally?[22] One historian has stressed the endemic nature of violence in Irish history;[23] another suggests that it has been exaggerated to the detriment of the Irish parliamentary tradition.[24] Whatever the merits of these contending views it is indisputable that, paradoxically, the security response adopted by the authorities has contributed mightily to paramilitary recruitment and civilian reluctance to inform on their own people.

The security response

> Killing a man is murder unless you do it to the sound of trumpets.
> Voltaire[25]

> You're giving them tea now. What will you be giving them in six months?
> Bernadette Devlin[26]

The British Army came on to the streets of Belfast and Derry to relieve an exhausted and discredited police force. It was ill-equipped for a long-term operation. It is one of only two wholly volunteer professional forces in Europe: Britain has – apart from Canada – the smallest percentage of its men of military age in uniform in NATO. It has withstood twenty years of manpower and equipment cuts, and while the bulk of its postwar operations involved it in the type of 'low intensity' conflicts such as Ulster, it was not properly trained to handle a policy of civilian control. Its immediate problem was lack of local intelligence but as that improved so did its difficulties with the local population: 'Cabinet must now discuss the constitutional consequences of the involvement of British troops. I don't think we can get them out of Northern Ireland at all easily now that they have gone into Belfast . . . I fear that once the Catholics and Protestants get used to our presence they will hate us more than they will hate each other.'[27]

Crossman's words were prophetic. The Army was ideal for short-term containment while the politicians conjured up the solutions, but when these did not appear Army/civilian relations grew sour. Soldiers were prime targets for IRA marksmen: in propaganda terms a soldier's death counted much more highly than that of a civilian, and in Ulster the Army suffered greater losses than 'in colonial-type policing in Palestine, Cyprus or Kenya. Only the Korean War and a thirteen year security operation in Malaya have cost the British more lives since 1945'.[28] In fact this strategy appears to be paying dividends. Since June 1974 British opinion has been consistent and clear: in each of nine surveys a majority has favoured a phased withdrawal of troops.[29]

With such casualties the temptation to get results by almost any means became a very high priority, and a premium was put on improving local intelligence. Hence increasing house searches: 'It was announced in Stormont (13 January 1972) that 1,183 houses and flats in Belfast had been searched by security forces between 30 November 1971 and 9 January 1972. In 47 of them arms, ammunition and radio equipment were found.'[30] That leaves 1,136 residences where nothing was found. At the very least we can assume that some householders resented these searches and that it is more than possible that excitable squaddies antagonised the occupants by treating them roughly, thereby acting as recruiting agents for the IRA.

Riot control agents such as CS gas also antagonised local communities. Here the problem was the indiscriminate nature of the device. When it was used to break up a riotous assembly, it was likely to seep into the houses of the area where the most vulnerable, the very young, the old and the bed-ridden could not make their escape. Similar problems were found with rubber bullets which were introduced to undo the harm of lead bullets. They were also found to be not altogether accurate and in 13 instances they proved lethal.

More pertinently, it was 'the nature of the Army as a closed institution unaccustomed to direct contact with the civilian population' which 'increased the likelihood that individual soldiers would be guilty of misconduct ... Individual soldiers ... soon realised that any breaches of discipline would be concealed by their colleagues or condoned by their officers'.[31] This aspect of Army activity was a continuing running sore. Michael McKeown calculated that 100 non-combatant fatalities were attributable to the security forces, and in only seven of these cases were charges brought against the soldiers: at the time of writing he found that only three cases had been disposed of.[32] One was acquitted, one got three years' imprisonment which was quashed on appeal, and one got one year's imprisonment for accidentally discharging his rifle while on sentry duty.

The most notorious case concerned the events of Bloody Sunday. Not only were no soldiers charged but Lt Col. Derek Wilford, the officer in charge of operations on that day, was awarded an OBE in the succeeding New Year's Honours List. To compound the insult the official enquiry, the Widgery Tribunal, proved to be a whitewash:

> Despite the attempts of the Widgery Tribunal to place the blame equally on both marchers and the Army, the facts, as stated by the tribunal itself, indicate that the Army, in an effort to capture members of the IRA, acted in a murderous and wholly unjustified fashion. . . . In all instances of factual discrepancies, facts must be weighed carefully; in this instance, Widgery to the contrary notwithstanding, the scales were tilted heavily against the Army's version of the events that led to the tragedy.[33]

So the judiciary was on trial as well as Army misconduct . . . and that could add to a contempt for parliamentary democracy which, in the long term, could be more debilitating than violence itself. Nor would it suffice to argue that the Provisionals were guilty of greater atrocities such as bombings in Birmingham (November 1974) and London (July 1982). The crucial point is that IRA members can be brought to justice: it is doubtful if the same holds for the Army.

Finally one set of events raises questions about the Army's political partiality, and that concerns its handling of the UWC strike in May 1974. Its intelligence operation could be faulted in not anticipating the enormity of the Protestant backlash: its relative sympathy for that community can be explained by the fact that only two of its 214 deaths could be blamed on Loyalists. But the decision that it could not stop the strike with the principle of minimum force 'was a profoundly important moment for it was the first time in two decades that a British Minister had been told by the Army that it could not cope with large-scale non-violent civil disturbance'. Additionally, 'many officers made up their minds, quite consciously, that Rees and Orme were incapable of controlling the UWC or of setting up and supporting political institutions which were worth defending.'[34]

All of the above is not to suggest that the Army will play an interventionist role on the mainland in some future 'doomsday scenario'. In fact, the Army has learnt a little modesty in Ulster, having a sneaking professional respect for the IRA's durability and being conscious of the difficulties of managing a complex technological society. Nor is it to imply that the Army's role in Ulster has been negative and purely destructive. The fundamental point to bear in mind is that there are two warring factions in Ulster who are capable of reducing the province to a desert. It is impossible to quantify the Army's protective capacity but it is reasonable to assume that it has prevented a bloodbath, a fact acknowledged even by many of those who call for its withdrawal. So the Army finds itself in the paradoxical position of being a major constraint on violence by using the very methods which encourage violence.

The low morale of the indigenous security forces added to the Army's difficulties. Relations between it and the RUC were not at all easy. The police have never reasserted the same authority they had in Ulster before 1968. Condemnatory remarks in the Cameron and Scarman Reports about some sections of the force gave credence to Republican propaganda that, in essence, the police were a partisan force. The publication of the Hunt Report in October 1969 spelt out the extent to which the RUC was a paramilitary force. Hunt ran counter to the accepted wisdom on internal security in Ireland since 1800. It envisaged the RUC becoming an unarmed civilian police service like any other in the United Kingdom and it tried to distance the police from the Unionist government by establishing an impartial Police Authority. The folly of Hunt was realised within the year. Northern Ireland patently was not like the

Home Counties. The police were soon rearmed as the battle with the IRA stepped up, but were forced to adopt a much more evenhanded approach to security duties. It underwent a radical transformation in image and personnel but still found it impossible to win the support of the Catholic minority. Only in the past few years have some elected Catholic representatives given even a grudging acceptance to the police. This has arisen because the RUC has demonstrated its willingness to take on the Loyalist paramilitaries as keenly as it desires to lock up Republicans.

The Government's decision to disband the 'B' Specials and replace them by a new part-time force under the command of the GOC produced the greatest bitterness in Loyalist circles. They saw this move as totally denuding them of security control. In time, however, they have placed their trust in the new regiment, the Ulster Defence Regiment (UDR). It began operations on 1 January 1970 and has acted as a valuable prop to an already stretched British Army because it has the capacity to do the work of almost four regiments. It was not expected to mirror the 'B' Specials although about 50 per cent of its first intake came from that source. An encouraging feature of that recruitment was that 18 per cent of the applicants were Catholics, and that 1,888 applicants have been refused admission to the force 'for security reasons'. That has not prevented the UDR acquiring a sectarian tinge. No less than 108 former UDR officers had been convicted of serious offences including sectarian assassinations by January 1976. Additionally Catholic membership in the force had dropped to just over 200 out of 7,835 enrolled members, largely as a result of an IRA campaign of intimidation.

It is impossible to quantify the effects of the 'security response'. The IRA started with an overall advantage insofar as the local security forces were detested by the Catholic population. Furthermore they were assisted by many Army activities, especially the internment debacle and the proven use of physical ill-treatment which followed. The Army was a clumsy device to use within the United Kingdom and did not always work within the constraints imposed by liberal democracy. And yet Ulster has avoided the ravages of Lebanon. It may be that we have not been reduced to a wasteland by the presence of these forces. Whatever be the truth, 'security' still remains part of the problem.

The search for consensus

> Sir, the state in choosing men to serve them takes no notice of their opinions: if they be willing faithfully to serve them, that satisfies.
>
> Oliver Cromwell, March 1644

When the Army moved in to Belfast in August 1969 Richard Crossman recorded in his diary that the action might have some advantages for the Government. 'It has deflected attention from our own deficiencies and the mess of the pound. We have now got into something which we can hardly mismanage.'[35] Looking at Whitehall policy over the past decade it is tempting to imagine that Crossman's views were pretty common among Ministers and civil servants. But that would be to oversimplify. The simple fact is that the Ulster problem is so complex and so intractible that a solution appears to be beyond the grasp of even the most fairminded and dedicated politician.

This brief section sums up the drift of the chapter by suggesting why the official British attitude has not been altogether helpful. Britain has seen its role in an altruistic light, that of a neutral but enlightened arbiter come among the combatants to offer succour and statecraft. It has forgotten that it is one of those combatants. It began by offering protection to the beleaguered Catholics, then to remove what it saw as parasitic aberrations, the IRA and other paramilitary groups; having failed to reform the Stormont system satisfactorily, to remove it temporarily while it educated the population in the virtues of parliamentary democracy; and finally, all else having failed, to emphasise its own statesmanlike qualities and its vast experience of governance in hostile environments. We have seen that its policies combined both coercion and conciliation but that by 1984 a solution seems as unattainable as ever.

There are two fundamental reasons why Britain's role can only be of limited assistance. Firstly our masters suffer from 'a blinkered empiricism, a philosophical and political narrowness of imagination about the passions that can move men in politics'.[36]

Secondly, the Ulster problem does not fit into the usual parameters of British political practice because 'in Ulster, the great, permanent question of political philosophy – the moral basis of authority, and of the right to resist authority, the relationship between law and force and that between nationality and political allegiance – were being debated.'[37]

In addition the Ulster problem is an Irish problem. Partition did not lessen Irish mythology about the indivisibility of the island but it did create an independent State which has nurtured its own vested interests ever since 1921. The Irish authorities, too, have wavered between coercion and conciliation so that by 1979 their policy could be summed up as 'British withdrawal but not yet, O Lord, not yet.'

If any lesson can be drawn from events over the past decade it must be that all parties to the problem – London, Dublin and the two Ulster communities – need to cooperate to find peace. Lloyd George did not conjure the Irish Question out of existence in 1921. It was still there in 1984, an Anglo-Irish problem largely fought on Ulster soil. But there has been more political movement recently than at any time since the 1920s. Proper time scales and concerned speculation are beginning to yield a richer harvest than mere reactive politics. It is time that that under-rated quality, prudence, began to play its part.

8 Elements of a Solution?

If we want a change in the attitude of Ireland we must begin by changing
our own.

J. R. Clynes MP[1]

Just as in the Republic the aspiration to acquire Northern Ireland is a low-
intensity aspiration, so in Great Britain the aspiration to get rid of
Northern Ireland is a low-intensity aspiration. Both have therefore low
priorities in terms of practical politics.

Conor Cruise O'Brien, June 1978

One of the reasons why political thinking is especially difficult in Ireland
is not (or not chiefly) that there is hatred between some few Catholics and
some few Protestants (and *vice versa*, God knows): it is that thinking is
stifled by myth, by the feeling that it is already too late for thought –
Nature has thought it out already.

Denis Donoghue[2]

Optimism is a rare commodity in Northern Ireland, for patently
obvious reasons. By October 1983 unemployment stood at 21·5 per
cent (the UK figure was 13 per cent). There is little consolation in
reflecting that the province has lived a permanent recession – never
as bleak as the present, it needs to be said – nor that current
unemployment is spreading the burden more equitably. While
Strabane in the west has over 40 per cent out of work some of the
more traditionally 'prosperous' eastern towns now have 25 per cent
unemployed. Those who believe that shared redundancy will unite
the working class do not know their Irish history; and even if
political leadership could agree on a common economic package it
does not have the muscle to move Whitehall.

That may seem to play into the IRA's hands. After all, they
received surprising popular endorsement in the wake of the hunger
strike. That campaign led to a fundamental reappraisal of strategy
and the perception that the military struggle could not succeed without political backup. Engagement in a mass movement (the 'H

Block' campaign) enabled them to make the psychological jump from the interstices of a sect to the glare of the international media. Thus the decision to contest the Assembly elections of October 1982 concurred with party strategy as announced in the party organ: 'The essence of republican struggle must be in armed resistance coupled with popular opposition to the British presence. So, while not everyone can plant a bomb, everyone can plant a vote.'[3] Such unambivalent militance paid dividends when PSF won five of the 78 seats and indeed secured more first preference votes (10·1 per cent) at the APNI (9·3 per cent).

These gains were consolidated at the General Election of June 1983 when the party vice-president, Gerry Adams, won Belfast West on an abstentionist ticket, and the other candidates passed the PSF target vote of 100,000 votes with 13·4 of the poll. Now they challenge the SDLP which they see as the greatest threat to their aspiration to lead the nationalist community.

The democratic parties may welcome PSF participation in the electoral process. Some optimists believe that this strategy will engender deep ideological divisions within the movement creating an irreconcilable split between the 'politicos' and the 'militants'. Some take comfort from the knowledge that growing abhorrence at the moral blackmail engaged in during the hunger strike led to a spate of information from the nationalist community. Others read their history more closely and remember the traumatic general election of 1918 when constitutional nationalism was swept to one side by a militant Sinn Fein capitalising on nationalist alienation.

We noted earlier the constraints placed on Loyalist terrorism. At times they exhibit a horrific capacity for indiscriminate sectarian assassination and a more controlled campaign against specific targets: in February 1981, for example, gunmen seriously injured Bernadette McAliskey (née Devlin) and her husband in front of their children. But generally they fit the description given them by the UDA commander, Andy Tyrie, as 'counter-terrorists'. That encapsulates their tendency to react to republican violence and acknowledges police success in the war of attrition.

Indeed, the UDA leadership has been engaged in a search for a political role and now advocates an independent Ulster based on the need to develop a separate economic strategy and an identity which is neither British nor Irish.[4] Meanwhile they founded a new party, the Ulster Loyalist Democratic Party, in June 1981. The ULDP may find that, like the Workers' Party, the road from terrorism to parliamentarism is strewn with unhappy reminders of a violent past. The latter, grown out of the Official IRA, has made a sustained and genuine effort to offer nonsectarian class politics to Northern Ireland with very little return for its efforts. Yet both parties have exercised a moderating influence on the wilder shores of working-class politics.

If extremism be judged on decibel level, Ian Paisley is champion. Until the Assembly elections his appeared a remarkable ascent of the greasy pole, from a by-election victory in April 1970 to near equality with the powerful UUP. His personal success in the direct elections to the European Parliament in June 1981 (when the province was treated as a single constituency and he took almost 30 per cent of the first preference votes) enhanced his messianic fervour: he interpreted the result as a 'twentieth-century miracle' engineered by the mysterious providence of God. Paisleyism and Provisionalism are symbiotic. They feed off each other and flourish in a climate of political and spiritual uncertainty. Both are anti-establishment, and both offer simplistic solutions to complex problems. But the former normally operates within the political process, whereas the latter has no such pretensions. Indeed both may share a cynicism about politics with a profound impatience for its constraints. Paisley, for example, has schemed legitimately to over-throw every Unionist leader since 1968, but has coalesced with the paramilitaries as well. In May 1977, with UDA assistance, he led an unsuccessful 'constitutional stoppage' to persuade the authorities to go on the offensive against the IRA and to restore Stormont. Loyalist indifference and decisive leadership defeated this attempt. (Incidentally, police determination to face up to Loyalist thuggery helped to win back tacit Catholic support.)

Paisley launched a second, more sinister, offensive in November 1981 following the Provo assassination of Rev. Robert Bradford. On this occasion he called for the dismissal of the Chief Constable, threatened to make Northern Ireland 'ungovernable' during a day of action on 23 November, and to make local government unworkable through boycott. In addition he formed a 'Third Force' ostensibly to complement the official security effort. This group of hooded men waving gun licences for the benefit of the media on lonely hills at the dead of night combined menace with absurdity. As Anglo-Irish relations developed Paisley embarked on the 'Carson Trail' drawing parallels with the dark days of 1912. Assuming the mantle of Sir Edward Carson he signed a contemporary version of the Ulster Declaration at Belfast City Hall on 9 February 1982, and offered his Third Force to protect loyal citizens from the IRA.

'Parson Carson's' reading of history was poor. In 1912 Unionists had established a powerful alliance with the Tories and made much of their respectability. Ian Paisley had placed himself so far beyond the pale of Westminster that Enoch Powell described him as 'the most resourceful, inveterate and dangerous enemy of the Union . . . a greater danger to the Union than the Foreign Office and the Provisional IRA rolled into one.'[5] The United States State Department seemed to concur with this view in December 1981 when they revoked his visa because they were concerned about the 'divisiveness' of his actions and statements which, they believed, were 'completely contrary to the interests of the UK in advancement of a peaceful settlement of the problem in Northern Ireland'.

Some Loyalist voters may have been influenced by these attitudes, because support has begun to slip away from the DUP in recent elections. The mainstream Unionists won five more seats than the DUP at the Assembly elections (26 to 21) in October 1982, and by June 1983 the Democratic Unionists were trailing by 14 per cent of the total poll and won only three of the 17 Westminister seats to the UUP's 11. Yet it would be very foolish to dismiss Paisleyism. Despite bluff and bluster Ian Paisley is not the Grand Old Duke of York. He has undoubted charisma and the most effective 'religio-political' machine in these islands. So long as constitutional uncertainty reigns and the security question is paramount, his brand of fundamentalism will present a threat. There are some policy-makers who continue to insist on the predominance of the security response; they do not stop to consider whether it is cause or effect. They can point to considerable security successes but are slower to respond to criticisms of its alienating effects. It may be that they are blinded by the mystique of professionalism. Since the mid-'70s a policy of 'Ulsterisation' has been implemented. Now a reformed RUC plays the dominant role and the Army simply lends support. A retrained and re-equipped police force assumed formal responsi-bility for security in January 1977 and has striven to live down its sectarian image. Allegations of police brutality have diminished since the Bennett Report[6] advocated reforms in interrogation methods. That is not to maintain that the security response no longer provokes controversy in the ghettoes. A running complaint in both communities has been RUC use of the evidence of 'converted terrorists' – or, to be blunt, 'super-grasses'. Uncorroborated evidence from this source before a judge sitting without a jury is seen by some as 'the latest instalment in a long line of security policies which have failed to eliminate political violence from this society.'[7] Undoubtedly super-grass evidence has dealt a severe blow to terrorist organisations in the short term but there is the more insidious danger that it might bring the legal process into greater contempt.

All of the above is depressing reading, but realistic. That is not to say that there is no light. After fifty years of stagnation Ulster has thrown the constitution-maker once more into a frenzy. Three attempts at internal settlement (Sunningdale, the Convention and the Atkins initiative), all based on power-sharing or its modification, have faltered on the majoritarian altar. The present Prior initiative is a minimalist plan based on 'acceptance' rather than 'reconciliation'. It has the merit of flexibility and will progress only as 'cross-community agreement' is arrived at. The first stage was the election to the 78-seat Assembly in October 1982, but since anti-partitionists adopted an abstentionist stance only 59 (Unionist) members took their seats. They have been invested with a scrutiny and consultative role. They have set up scrutiny committees for each of the six Stormont departments and use the Assembly to discuss local legislation. They have succeeded in making direct rule more accountable. Yet there is little possibility of movement towards a second stage whereby one or more local departments could embrace devolution since the DUP and UUP with 47 seats will not countenance any form of power-sharing. In fact the evidence would suggest that the latter are becoming integrationist and may not believe in the efficacy of a local legislature. Initially the party boycotted the committee system and by November 1983 their commitment appeared less than total.

It is conceivable but unlikely that if the SDLP entered the Assembly it could move towards a devolved stage. That party's abstention is based on the belief that the initiative is unworkable because it ignores the 'broader dimensions of the problem'. SDLP thinking is dominated by the Irish dimension and British-Irish cooperation. Mr Prior's 'rolling devolution' can build that into the model but again only if there is some cross-community support. In the interim officials have begun to examine the 'broader dimensions . . .'.

It is only when we set the problem in this wider context that tentative hope arises. Policy makers, blinded by the transient success of Sunningdale, tried to achieve a solution before even defining the parameters of the problem. It has taken more than 800 years of Anglo-Irish hostility to bring together British and Irish officials to analyse 'the reasons for misconceptions in each country over attitudes and Government policies in the other' and to consider 'measures which the two Governments might take, jointly or separately, to remove such misconceptions and improve mutual misunderstanding'.[8] It took 14 years of unmitigated conflict in Northern Ireland and international pressure to persuade the sovereign powers that there are benefits in security and functional cooperation. Now they are beginning to face up to their considerable responsibilities.

Security cooperation has been the most practical manifestation of the mutuality of the problem. After initial suspicions were overcome the Garda and RUC work very closely together.[9] Although Dublin continues to refuse to extradite alleged political offenders (citing the difficulties inherent in amending a written Constitution), she has passed a Criminal Law Jurisdiction Act (1976) whereby criminals can be tried in the Republic for offences committed in the United Kingdom. The first convictions were secured in December 1981 when Provisionals who had escaped from Belfast's Crumlin Road prison were sentenced to ten years' imprisonment in Dublin. A more historic judgement was the sentence of Gerard Tuite on evidence from New Scotland Yard in Dublin in July 1982 on a charge of possessing explosives in London. Now that it has been established that no one is immune from arrest within the British Isles, huge pressure is placed on the terrorists. This cooperation has extended to the United States where a better informed Irish-American electorate has withdrawn much of its emotional and financial support from the IRA. Succesive Taoisigh and particularly the leader of the SDLP, John Hume, must take the credit for this massive task of political education. Patronising British spokesmen and moralising newspaper editors could never have had the same effect.

Another practical advantage has been functional cooperation. Historically Anglo-Irish relations have been unequal, so much so that Ireland's dependence on Britain was incompatible with the status of political sovereignty. Her 'economic miracle' of the 1960s and accession to the EEC has changed all that. Her dependence on the United Kingdom is diminishing – by 1981 it 'was the destination of 43 per cent of our exports as against 55 per cent in 1973, whereas the Continental EEC takes 32 per cent as against 21 per cent . . .'[10] EEC membership has given the Republic coordinate, and not subordinate, status with Britain. It has allowed her an international forum to establish a more friendly relationship with her traditional enemy, and has raised hopes that it might improve relations within the island: '. . . in the context of the EEC, there is a clear opportunity for developing cooperation on economic and social issues which could bring considerable benefits to the people in both the North and South of Ireland.'[11] Those hopes have not been fully realised, nor has social and economic cooperation always run on straight tracks, but at least by 1980 the 'complex interdependence' of the problem had been recognised by Dublin and London.

This followed a summit meeting in London between the two Prime Ministers, Margaret Thatcher and Charles Haughey, on 21 May 1980. They agreed to meet regularly and to develop a closer political cooperation. The next meeting was held in Dublin on 8 December where, according to the Taoiseach, the 'British delegation was, in terms of its composition, the most important to visit this country since the foundation of the State or indeed for a long time before then'. They acknowledged that substantial progress had been made in those few months in the fields of energy, transport, communications, cross-border economic development and security; and they decided that senior officials of the two governments should undertake joint studies covering possible new institutional structures, citizenship rights, security matters, economic cooperation and measures to encourage mutual understanding. The process was taken a stage further at the summit on 6 November 1981 when the new Taoiseach, Garret FitzGerald, and Mrs Thatcher announced the establishment of an Anglo-Irish Council. (Dr FitzGerald formed a coalition government in June after the Fianna Fail government lost the general election on its economic policies. His government was to collapse within seven months as the recession bit harder in the Irish Republic).

The first meeting of a new Anglo-Irish Inter-Governmental Council took place in London on 29 January 1982. The next summit did not occur until 7 November 1983 at Chequers. During that period the AIIC had twenty bilateral meetings at Ministerial level and had discussed a wide range of political, economic and cultural matters and had developed economic cooperation. In particular progress was made in the energy field after an agreement was signed on 10 October 1983 to supply natural gas from the Kinsale field in the Republic to Northern Ireland over a 22-year period.

None of this, however, could disguise the fact that the Anglo-Irish process had ground to a jarring halt for almost two years, the victim of misunderstanding, national psyches and geopolitics. The basic reason lay in the counter-claims of the respective domestic jurisdictions. For example, the December 1980 summit was shrouded in secrecy and yet the joint communique referred to the 'totality of relationships within these islands'. That was open to misinterpretation. Ian Paisley launched his Carson Trail and Charles Haughey, aware that a deteriorating economy challenged his government majority, tried to hype the significance of summitry. During 1981 the hunger strike put tremendous strain on the Irish Government to force concessions out of Mrs Thatcher. Finally the Falklands crisis and Ireland's insistence on exercising her sovereignty within the EEC (by opposing trade sanctions against Argentina) undermined that phase of Anglo-Irish relations. All of this bears out the sensitive nature of such a process and the historical legacy which it carries:

> Britain is engrossed with an immediate problem. She assumes a common war effort because there is a common general interest. She sees herself as readily forgiving past transgressions, and therefore entitled to ready pardon. But these are not pleas which can be heard clearly by Irish ears. They are drowned or distorted by the noises of old coercion, old condescension, old colonialism, and old battles for parity and the rule of ordinary law.[12]

Ireland, too, has been engrossed with immediate problems, most of which were self-inflicted. The most theatrical was a campaign to insert an amendment into the Constitution which would protect the life of the unborn, this in a country which outlawed abortion. It led to a long and divisive debate, and was followed by a Constitutional referendum which voted two to one in favour of such a move, although there was a high abstention rate.

All of this was proceeding while the New Ireland Forum, a body composed of the Republic's three major parties and the SDLP, met in 1983 to engage in a rigorous exercise of self-analysis: nothing less than the removal of the Catholic and Gaelic ethos from the 1937 Constitution to make a new Ireland more attractive to northern Protestants. It was a recognition that Dublin's claim on Northern Ireland had been aspirational rather than operational, and that it was based on the passive policy of a solution being found 'in the larger general play of English interest'. Such soul-searching can be beneficial; at the very least it indicates that intelligent speculation can replace reactive emotionalism.

But intelligent speculation can take time, especially as it has to overcome the political mythology of the 60 years since Ireland was partitioned. The Forum first met in public session on 30 May 1983, when the leaders of the two government parties, Dr Garret FitzGerald of Fine Gael and Dick Spring of the Labour Party, the leader of the major opposition party, Charles Haughey of Fianna Fail, and John Hume, leader of the SDLP, put forward their thoughts on the shape of a new Ireland. They represented, of course, constitutional nationalism, but their opening addresses indicated that there was no consensus on the way forward. Thus their original timetable, which called for a detailed Report before the end of the year, proved over-optimistic.

In fact, the final Report did not appear until 2 May 1984, after a total of 28 private sessions, 13 public sessions, 56 meetings of a Steering Group, and numerous meetings of subgroups which examined economic issues and alternative constitutional structures in detail. Those structures concentrated on models of a unitary state, a federal/confederal state and a system of joint authority whereby London and Dublin would have equal responsibility for the government of Northern Ireland. The general tenor of the Report, however, favoured a unitary state, partly as a gesture to traditional Fianna Fail policy but actually in obeisance to the aspirational rather than the operational.

Indeed the Report was more subtle than instant comment suggested. For example, para. 5.6 spoke of the necessity to 'achieve

Irish unity in agreement', and of the six structures of political unity presented no less than three were examples of federal states (Australia, Switzerland and the United States). In reality, the Report has to be seen as a negotiating document in the ongoing Anglo-Irish process. To that extent it is an acknowledgement of the many unpalatable realities to which the Forum addressed itself. Whereas Unionist parties refused to play any role in the proceedings, individual Unionists and the Conservative MP, Sir John Biggs-Davison, were eloquent in defending the Union and in presenting Unionist perceptions of nationalist threats. Of equal significance was evidence presented by the major Protestant churches in Ireland and a searching analysis of the role of the Catholic church in shaping modern Ireland.

At the end of the day the Report is a *nationalist* Report, replete with a nationalist interpretation of Irish history. But there is in it an honest acceptance that partition can only be overcome through consent. Initial Loyalist reaction indicates that consent will not be forthcoming. The Unionist Party orchestrated a pre-emptive strike with the publication, some days before that of the Forum, of 'Devolution and the Northern Ireland Assembly: The Way Forward'. This paper forecast the failure of the Forum strategy, suggested that reconciliation should be attempted from the bottom up and not from the top down, offered administrative devolution and a Bill of Rights. The DUP was characteristically more hostile: its document, 'The Unionist Case – the Forum Report Answered', concluded that such 'is the antipathy of Northern Unionists to Irish unification that even if the alternative was to eat grass and die, they would sooner die'.

Reaction from the Secretary of State was more muted but mildly optimistic. The Government would study the Report with an open mind and respond in due course, and was prepared to debate the Report in the House. Here was some recognition that something more than mere reaction to political violence was essential. In that respect they were following the lead of others. The British Labour Party in 1981, for example, endorsed a policy statement by its executive which states that 'our policy should be based on the objective of unity between the two parts of Ireland', an objective to be realised only with the consent of the people of Northern Ireland. *The Guardian* has speculated on the concept of the Islands of the

North Atlantic.[13] Academics have been thinking aloud about federation, confederation and condominium.[14] The time has come for Government representatives to consider the mote in their own jurisdiction as well as the beam in their neighbours'.

Whether or not any of these ideas can contribute to resolving Northern Ireland's problems, they will take a long time to come to fruition. For the moment, in place of optimism there is despair, and, with more than 2,300 violent deaths and proportionally the largest prison population in Western Europe, Northern Ireland cannot afford that.

Notes and references

Chapter 1. The Genesis of the Ulster Crisis: Themes and Myths

1. C. Smyth, *Rome – Our Enemy* (Puritan Publishing Co., 1984), p. 13. The author was a member of the Rev. Ian Paisley's Democratic Unionist Party and Secretary of the United Ulster Unionist Council in 1974.
2. Quoted in Ruth Dudley Edwards, *Patrick Pearse: The Triumph of Failure* (Gollancz, 1977), p. 191. Patrick Pearse led the 1916 Rising in Dublin. The Provisional IRA claim him as their secular saint.
3. H. Tudor, *Political Myth* (Pall Mall, 1972), p. 138.
4. M. W. Heslinga, *The Irish Border as a Cultural Divide* (Van Gorcum, Assen, 1971), p. 154.
5. E. Estyn Evans, 'The personality of Ulster', *Transactions of the Institute of British Geographers*, 1970, p. 4.
6. Smyth, *op cit.*, p. 25.
7. James Connolly, *Labour in Irish History* (Three Candles, 1910), pp. 79–80. Connolly was a socialist and trade union organiser who had worked in both Belfast and Dublin. His Citizen's Army fought alongside Patrick Pearse in 1916.
8. Cited in Conor Cruise O'Brien, *States of Ireland* (2nd edn, Panther, 1974), p. 44.
9. Cited in *Ireland: Two Nations*, (British and Irish Communist Organisation, 1971).
10. Paul Bew, 'The problem of Irish unionism', *Economy and Society*, 6(1), 1977, p. 99.
11. I. Budge and C. O'Leary, *Belfast: Approach to Crisis* (Macmillan, 1973), p. 107.
12. Cited in Peter Gibbon, *The Origins of Ulster Unionism* (Manchester University Press, 1974), p. 126.
13. O'Brien, *op. cit.*, p. 29.
14. Frank Wright, 'Protestant ideology and politics in Ulster', *European Journal of Sociology* XIV, 1973, pp. 233–34.
15. Gibbon, *op. cit.*, p. 23.
16. See J. H. Whyte, 'Catholic–protestant relations in countries other than Ireland', J. B. Earley (ed.), *Sectarianism – Roads to Reconciliation* (Three Candles, 1974), pp. 14–24.
17. *Belfast Newsletter*, 15 May 1861. Cited in Wright, *op. cit.*, p. 224.

18. Owen Dudley Edwards, *Irish Times*, 22 March 1973.
19. Nicholas Mansergh, *The Irish Question, 1840–1921* (Unwin, 1965), pp. 195–6.
20. Liam de Paor, *Irish Times*, 18 January 1977.
21. Brian Inglis, *Roger Casement* (Hodder and Stoughton, 1973), p. 232.
22. Winston Churchill, *The Aftermath* (Odhams, 1929), p. 283.
23. Tudor, *op. cit.*, p. 139.

Chapter 2. A 'Decorative' Constitution

1. S. Andreski, *Parasitism and Subversion*, (Weidenfeld and Nicholson, 1966). p. 125.
2. F. F. Ridley, *The Study of Government* (Allen and Unwin, 1975), p. 21.
3. *New Statesman*, 19 July 1974.
4. HC Deb., vol. 127, cols 976–7.
5. Nicholas Mansergh, *The Government of Northern Ireland. A Study in Devolution* (Allen and Unwin, 1936), p. 314. Italics added.
6. Claire Palley, *The Evolution, Disintegration and Possible Reconstruction of the Northern Ireland Constitution* (Barry Rose Publishers, 1973), p. 389.
7. See HC Deb. (NI), vol. 2, col. 226.
8. In some of the dependent territories of the Empire where differences of race and culture were often sharp, Britain thought in terms of the 'claims of communities' rather than individuals. See Vernon Van Dyke, 'One man, one vote and majority rule as human rights', *Revue des Droits de l'Homme*, VI, 3–4.
9. Enoch Powell MP, addressing Unionists in Co. Tyrone, 11 September 1971.
10. T. E. Utley, *Lessons of Ulster* (Dent, 1975), p. 17.
11. HC Deb. (NI), vol. 1, col. 1974.
12. *Northern Whig*, 6 April 1925.
13. Geoffrey Bing, *Irish Times*, 24 December 1973.
14. P. Bew and P. Gibbon, 'Stormont and the minority in the inter-war period', paper read at Conference of Irish Historians, Coleraine, May 1977, pp. 7, 8 and 17.
15. Richard Rose, *Governing Without Consensus* (Faber, 1971), p. 73.
16. Brian Farrell, *The Irish Parliamentary Tradition* (Gill and Macmillan, 1973), pp. 213–14.
17. C. E. B. Brett, 'The lesson of devolution in Northern Ireland', *Political Quarterly*, 14, 1970, p. 273.
18. F. S. L. Lyons, *Ireland Since The Famine* (Weidenfeld and Nicolson, 1971), p. 685.
19. *Report of the Advisory Committee on the Police*, Cmnd 535, 1969, para. 80.
20. Bew and Gibbon, *op. cit.*, pp. 4–6.

21. Cited in Palley, *op. cit.*, p. 401.
22. *Ibid.* p. 400.
23. J. C. Beckett, 'Northern Ireland', *Journal of Contemporary History*, 6(1), 1971, p. 124.
24. G. L. Dobbie, *Protectors and Partisans* (Conference on N.I., University of Lancaster, 1971).
25. Richard Rose, *Fortnight*, 115, p. 9.
26. *Ibid.* p. 12.
27. *Ibid.* p. 12.
28. Martin Wallace, *Northern Ireland: 50 Years of Self-Government* (David and Charles, 1971), p. 157.
29. *Ibid.* p. 158.
30. *Royal Commission on the Constitution 1969–1973*, Cmnd 5460 (October 1973) para. 1287; hereinafter known as the Kilbrandon Report.
31. G. C. Duggan, *Northern Ireland: Success or Failure?* (Irish Times, 1950), p. 7.
32. *The Banker*, September 1947, p. 179.
33. Carl Friederich, *Constitutional Government and Democracy* (New York, 1968), p. 171.

Chapter 3. A Divided Society

1. R. Harris, *Prejudice and Tolerance in Ulster* (Manchester University Press, 1972), p. 225.
2. E. McCann, *War and an Irish Town*, (Penguin, 1974), p. 9. The author was a civil rights activist in the late 1960s and a resident of the Catholic area of the Bogside in Derry.
3. Richard Rose, *Governing Without Consensus* (Faber, 1971), p. 445.
4. Harris, *op. cit.*, pp. 189–90.
5. D. P. Barritt and C. F. Carter. *The Northern Ireland Problem* (Oxford University Press, 1962), pp. 107–8.
6. Conor Cruise O'Brien, *States of Ireland* (2nd edn, Panther, 1974), p. 286.
7. A. Lijphart, 'Northern Ireland problem: cases, theories and solutions', *British Journal of Political Science*, 5, 1975, p. 87.
8. Billy Mitchell, a senior UVF man, quoted in *The Observer*, 3 August 1975.
9. Irate Protestant quoted in Harold Jackson, *The Two Irelands* (Minority Rights Group, 1971), p. 4.
10. Donald Akenson, *Education and Enmity* (David and Charles, 1973), p. 195.
11. Owen Dudley Edwards, *The Sins of Our Fathers* (Gill and Macmillan, 1970), pp. 64ff., p. 184.
12. J. Hickey, 'Religion As A Factor In Northern Ireland', *Social Studies*, Winter, 1976–77, p. 184.

13. F. Boal, *Community Forum*, 3, 1972, p. 10.
14. Harris, *op. cit.*, pp. 195–5 and *passim*.
15. Jackson, *op. cit.*, p. 6.
16. P. Buckland, 'The Unity of Ulster Unionism', *History*, 60, 1975, pp. 219–22.
17. Harris, *op. cit.*, p. 188.
18. R. Hauser, *A Social Option* (London, 1975), p. 81.
19. Cardinal MacRory, cited in the *Irish News*, 18 December 1931.
20. Michael Foy, 'The Ancient Order of Hibernians. A Religio-Political Pressure Group', unpublished MA thesis, Queen's University, Belfast (1976), *passim*.
21. J. H. Whyte, *Church and State in Modern Ireland 1923–1970* (Gill and Macmillan, 1971), p. 9.
22. E. Aunger, 'Religion and occupational class in Northern Ireland', *Economic and Social Reviews*, 7(1), p. 1 and *passim*.
23. *Ibid.* p. 5.
24. Harris, *op cit.*, p. 174.
25. *Ibid.* pp. 198–9.
26. Michael J. Murphy, *Tyrone Folk Quest*, (Blackstaff Press, 1973), p. 12.
27. P. Loizos and J. Bayley, *New Society*, 21 August 1969, p. 278.
28. R. Weiner, *The Rape and Plunder of the Shankill* (published by the author, Belfast, 1975), p. 76.
29. Harris, *op. cit.*, p. 168.
30. F. S. L. Lyons, *Ireland Since the Famine* (Weidenfeld and Nicolson, 1971), p. 746.
31. Barritt and Carter, *op. cit.*, p. 99.
32. E. McCann, *op. cit.*, p. 212.
33. Cited by D. W. Harkness, *Irish Times*, 21 April 1976.
34. Harris, *op. cit.*, p. 223.

Chapter 4. A 'Majority Dictatorship'?

1. A. J. Milner, *Elections and Political Stability* (Boston, 1969), p. 26.
2. Nationalist MP and leader of his party in the 1960s. The quotation appears in his pamphlet, *Irish Action* (Derry, 1948), p. 3.
3. Cited by Geoffrey Bing, *John Bull's Other Ireland* (*Tribune* pamphlet, 1950), p. 6.
4. Lord Craigavon, HC Deb. (NI), vol. 8, col. 2276.
5. R. Rose, *Governing Without Consensus* (Faber, 1971), p. 237.
6. R. Rose, *Northern Ireland: A Time of Choice* (Macmillan, 1976), p. 78.
7. Cornelius O'Leary, 'Belfast West', in D. Butler and A. King, *The British General Election of 1966* (London, 1966), p. 255.

8. Rose (1971), *op. cit.*, p. 219.

9. Rose (1976), *op. cit.*, p. 69.

10. D. P. Barritt and C. F. Carter, *The Northern Ireland Problem* (Oxford University Press, 1962), p. 44.

11. Quoted in J. A. V. Graham, 'The consensus-forming strategy of the Northern Ireland Labour Party, 1949–67', unpublished M.S.Sc. thesis, Queen's University, Belfast, (1974), p. 69.

12. Terence O'Neill, *Autobiography* (Hart-Davis, 1972), p. 75.

13. Interview, *Sunday Independent*, 16 November 1969.

14. E. McAteer, *Irish Action*, p. 4.

15. E. McCann, *War and an Irish Town* (Penguin, 1974), p. 11.

16. Rose (1971), *op. cit.*, p. 221.

17. McCann, *op. cit.*, pp. 12–13.

18. Michael Foy 'The Ancient Order of Hibernians. A Religio-Political Pressure Group', unpublished MA thesis, Queen's University, Belfast (1976), pp. 158–9.

19. I. McAllister, *The Northern Ireland Social Democratic and Labour Party: Political Opposition in a Divided Society* (Macmillan, 1977), p. 128.

20. *Ireland's Fascist City* (Derry, 1946).

21. McAllister, *op. cit.*, p. 19.

22. See J. A. V. Graham, *op. cit.*, p. 19.

23. See I. Budge and C. O'Leary, *Belfast: Approach to Crisis* (Macmillan, 1973), pp. 161–2.

24. Former Unionist MP, *Fortnight*, no. 73, 1973.

25. Former Prime Minister, quoted in W. H. Van Voris, *Violence in Ulster* (Amherst, 1975), p. 171.

26. See John F. Harbinson, *The Ulster Unionist Party* (Blackstaff Press, 1973), pp. 67–9.

27. *Ibid.* p. 95.

28. F. Wright, 'Protestant ideology and politics in Ulster', *European Journal of Sociology*, XIV, 1973, p. 248.

29. C. Smyth, *Rome – Our Enemy* (Puritan Publishing Co., 1974), p. 78.

30. R. Harris, *Prejudice and Tolerance in Ulster* (Manchester University Press, 1972), p. 187.

31. J. H. Whyte, 'Intra-Unionist disputes in the Northern Ireland House of Commons 1921–72', *Economic and Social Review*, 1973–74, pp. 94–104.

32. P. Bew, P. Gibbon, H. Patterson, *The State in Northern Ireland, 1921–72* (Manchester University Press, 1979), *passim*.

33. I. Budge and C. O'Leary, *op. cit.*, pp. 145ff.

34. C. O'Leary in Butler and King, *op. cit.*, p. 257.

35. A. Lijphart, 'Northern Ireland Problem: Cases, Theories and Solutions', *British Journal of Political Science*, 5, 1975, p. 95.

Chapter 5. A Devolved Administration

1. Unionist MP and President of the Belfast Chamber of Commerce, quoted in *The Banker*, September 1946, p. 162.
2. G. Fitzgerald, *Towards a New Ireland* (Temple Smith, 1972), p. 80. The author is leader of Fine Gael, the major opposition party in the Irish Republic.
3. T. K. Daniel, 'Griffith on his noble head: the determinants of Cumann na nGaedheal economic policy, 1922–32', *Irish Economic and Social History*, 1976, p. 60.
4. Liam de Paor, *Irish Times*, 8 December 1977.
5. E. Rumpf and A. C. Hepburn, *Nationalism and Socialism in twentieth-century Ireland* (Liverpool University Press, 1977), pp. 118–19.
6. Michael McInerney, *Irish Times*, 30 December 1977.
7. John A. Murphy, *Ireland in the Twentieth Century* (Gill and Macmillan, 1975), p. 90.
8. John A. Murphy, *Irish Times*, 30 December 1977.
9. Donal Barrington, *Uniting Ireland* (Tuairim pamphlet, Dublin, undated), p. 12.
10. Fitzgerald, *op. cit.*, p. 79.
11. A. H. Birch, *Political Integration and Disintegration in the British Isles* (Allen and Unwin, 1977), p. 83.
12. *A House Divided* (Collins, 1973), p. 2.
13. Paul Bew 'The Problem of Irish Unionism', *Economy and Society*, 6,(1), 1977, p. 107.
14. Kilbrandon Report, para. 1261.
15. See Norman Furniss, 'Northern Ireland as a case study of decentralization in unitary states', *World Politics*, 1975, *passim*, for a further discussion of Stormont's legislative record.
16. Terence O'Neill, *Autobiography* (Hart-Davis, 1972), p. 49.
17. C. Desmond Greaves, *The Irish Crisis* (Lawrence and Wishart, 1972), pp. 41–2.
18. See Kilbrandon Report, para. 166 and fn. 1, p. 139, for a United Kingdom comparison.
19. See K. S. Isles, *The Banker*, September 1948, pp. 179–84.
20. A. H. Birch, *op. cit.*, p. 34.
21. R. Davies and M. A. McGurnaghan, 'Northern Ireland: the economics of adversity', *National Westminster Bank Quarterly Review*, May 1975, p. 58.
22. Fair Employment Agency, 1978, pp. 6 and 13.
23. F. Wright, 'Protestant ideology in politics in Ulster', *European Journal of Sociology*, XIV, 1973, p. 264–5.
24. *Belfast Telegraph*, 3 August 1961.

25. O'Neill, *op. cit.*, p. 47.
26. Furniss, *op cit.*, pp. 396–7.
27. *Journal of the RIBA*, November 1949, p. 10.
28. Desmond Donnelly, *Official Architect*, December 1948, pp. 578–80.
29. Quoted in R. Weiner, *The Rape and Plunder of the Shankill* (published by the author, Belfast, 1975), p. 99.
30. Sir Ronald Nugent, Minister of Commerce, Cabinet memorandum, 6 January 1946, quoted in D. W. Harkness, *Irish Times*, 16 November 1977.
31. F. S. L. Lyons, *Ireland Since the Famine* (Weidenfeld and Nicolson, 1971), p. 729.
32. G. C. Duggan, *Northern Ireland: Success or Failure?* (Irish Times, 1950), p. 7.
33. D. Birrell and A. Murie, 'Ideology, conflict and social policy', *The Journal of Social Policy*, 1975, pp. 256–67.

Chapter 6. One Man One Vote

1. Televised broadcast, 9 December 1968.
2. *Belfast Telegraph*, 25 August 1978.
3. Louis McNeice, 'Belfast', *Collected Poems 1925–48* (Faber edition).
4. Terence O'Neill, *Autobiography* (Hart-Davis, 1972), p. 47.
5. Cornelius O'Leary, 'The Northern Ireland General Election (1969)', *Verfassung und Verfassungswirklichkeit* (Cologne and Opladen, 1969), p. 126.
6. *The Observer*, 19 April 1970.
7. W. R. Rodgers, Epilogue to 'The Character of Ireland', *Collected Poems* (Oxford, 1971), p. 147.
8. Richard Rose, *Governing Without Consensus* (Faber, 1971), p. 306.
9. Conor Cruise O'Brien, *States of Ireland* (2nd edn, Panther, 1974), p. 141.
10. I. McAllister, *The Northern Ireland Social Democratic and Labour Party: Political Opposition in a Divided Society* (Macmillan, 1977), p. 7.
11. Owen Dudley Edwards, *The Sins of our Fathers* (Gill and Macmillan, 1970), p. 246.
12. *Ibid.* p. 246.
13. Rex Cathcart, *Irish Times*, 16 March 1976.
14. *Belfast Telegraph*, 24 April 1967.
15. A. T. Q. Stewart, *The Narrow Ground* (Faber, 1977), p. 16.
16. Rose (1971), *op. cit.*, p. 306.
17. Brian Faulkner, *Memoirs of a Statesman* (Weidenfeld and Nicolson, 1978), p. 39–40.
18. V. S. Pritchett, *Midnight Oil* (Penguin, 1974), p. 114.
19. Quoted in David Boulton, *The UVF 1966–73* (Torc, 1973), p. 43.

20. Rose (1971), *op. cit.*, pp. 193 and 255.
21. Boulton, *op. cit.*, pp. 126–7.
22. R. Weiner, *The Rape and Plunder of the Shankill* (published by the author, Belfast, 1975), p. 57 and pp. 44–5.
23. F. Wright, 'Protestant ideology in politics in Ulster', *European Journal of Sociology*, XIV, 1973, p. 262.
24. O'Brien, *op. cit.*, pp. 140–1.
25. John Oliver, *Working at Stormont* (Institute of Public Administration, 1978), pp. 80 and 81.
26. Cited in Frank Gallagher, *The Indivisible Island* (Gollancz, 1959), p. 245.
27. Oliver, *op. cit.*, p. 90.
28. Faulkner, *op. cit.*, p. 72.
29. Interview with Terence O'Neill, *Belfast Telegraph*, 10 May 1969.
30. Wright, *op. cit.*, pp. 273–4.
31. Alan Robinson, 'Social and Economic Geography of Londonderry', unpublished MA thesis, Queen's University, Belfast, 1968.
32. A. T. Q. Stewart, *op. cit.*, p. 52.
33. *Disturbances in Northern Ireland* (Belfast, 1969) Cmnd 532. The Northern Ireland Government established – at London's behest – a Commission (headed by a Scottish judge, Lord Cameron) to enquire into the reasons for the outbreak of violence in Ulster after 5 October 1968.
34. I. Budge and C. O'Leary, *Belfast: Approach to Crises* (Macmillan, 1973), p. 177.
35. O'Brien *op. cit.*, p. 169.
36. O'Neill, *op. cit.*, p. 111.
37. Faulkner, *op. cit.*, p. 48.
38. Sarah Nelson, 'Developments in Protestant working-class politics', *Social Studies*, Winter, 1976–77, p. 207.
39. Vincent E. Feeney, 'The civil rights movements in Northern Ireland', *Eire-Ireland* 9(2), 1974, p. 36 and *passim*.
40. Conor Cruise O'Brien, 'Ireland and minority rights', *New Humanist*, March 1973, p. 434.

Chapter 7. A State of Emergency

1. Quoted by Nell McCafferty, *Irish Times*, 15 and 16 November 1971.
2. Richard Rose, *Northern Ireland: A Time of Choice* (Macmillan, 1976), p. 62.
3. Max Hastings, *Ulster 1969* (Gollancz, 1970), pp. 143–4.
4. Sir Kenneth Newman, Chief Constable RUC, *Sunday Times*, 22 October 1978.

5. John Whale, *Sunday Times*, 5 September 1976.

6. Letters, *The Times*, 26 November 1971.

7. On the work of the Executive see B. Faulkner, *Memoirs of a Statesman* (Weidenfeld and Nicolson, 1978), J. Oliver, *Working at Stormont* (Institute of Public Administration, Dublin, 1978), P. Devlin, *The Fall of the NI Executive* (published by the author, Belfast, 1975).

8. I. McAllister, *The Northern Ireland Social Democratic and Labour Party: Political Opposition in a Divided Society* (Macmillan, 1977), p. 159.

9. Seamus Heaney, 'Whatever You Say, Say Nothing', *North* (Faber, 1975), p. 59.

10. J. Darby and A. Williamson, *Violence and the Social Services* (Heinemann, 1978), Map III, p. 13.

11. Rose (1976), *op cit.*, pp. 24–5.

12. See 'The cost of violence arising from the Northern Ireland situation since 1969', *The New Ireland Forum* (Dublin, November 1983) and Norman Gibson, 'Violence and the Northern Ireland Economy', *Ireland Today*, September 1983.

13. H. A. Lyons, 'Riots and Rioters in Belfast', *Community Forum*, 3/2, 1973.

14. Hywel Griffith, in Darby and Williamson, *op. cit.*, p. 181.

15. E. McCann, *War and an Irish Town* (Penguin, 1974), pp. 78–9.

16. J. Bowyer Bell, *Review of Politics*, 1972, p. 402.

17. Conor Cruise O'Brien, *States of Ireland*, (2nd edn, Panther, 1974), p. 177.

18. J. Bowyer Bell, *op. cit.*, p. 409.

19. *Sunday Times* Insight Team, *Ulster* (London, 1972), p. 403.

20. Compiled from Appendix 13 of vol. 1, and Appendix 10 of vol. 3, R. Deutsch and V. Magowan, *Northern Ireland: Chronology of Events*, (Blackstaff Press, 1973, 1974 and 1975).

21. Denis Donoghue, 'Inside the Maze – legitimising heirs to the Men of 1916', *The Listener*, 3 September 1981, p. 227.

22. Richard Rose, Ian McAllister and Peter Mair, *Is there a Concurring Majority about Northern Ireland?* (Centre for the Study of Public Policy, 1978), p. 37.

23. A. T. Q. Stewart, *Narrow Ground* (Faber, 1977), pp. 113–22.

24. Brian Farrell (ed.), *The Irish Parliamentary Tradition* (Gill and Macmillan, 1973), *passim*.

25. Cited by Anthony Arblaster, *Political Studies*, XXV, 3, 1977, p. 413.

26. Speech in the Bogside, August 1969. Her remarks referred to the very warm welcome the Army received from the Catholic community. The Provisional IRA replied to her rhetorical question from late 1971 onwards.

27. Richard Crossman, 17 August 1969, *The Diaries of a Cabinet Minister*, vol. 3 (Cape, 1977).
28. Rose (1976), *op. cit.*, p. 62.
29. Richard Rose and Ian McAllister, *United Kingdom Facts* (Macmillan, 1982), p. 121.
30. Deutsch and Magowan, *op. cit.*, p. 149.
31. K. Boyle, T. Hadden and P. Hillyard, *Law and State: The Case of Northern Ireland* (Martin Robertson, 1975), p. 35.
32. Michael McKeown, *Hibernia*, 22 November 1974.
33. Roger H. Hull, *The Irish Triangle. Conflict in Northern Ireland* (Princeton University Press, 1976), pp. 88–9.
34. R. Fisk, *The Point of No Return* (Deutsch, 1975), p. 153 and pp. 230–1.
35. Richard Crossman, *op. cit.*, vol. 3, p. 620.
36. Bernard Crick, *Political Theory and Practice* (Allen Lane, 1972), p. 215.
37. T. E. Utley, *Lessons of Ulster* (Dent, 1975), p. 7.

Chapter 8. Elements of a solution?

1. HC Deb., vol. 127, ed. 955, speaking on the second reading of the Government of Ireland Bill, 1920.
2. *New Statesman*, 22 September 1978, p. 366.
3. *An Phoblacht*, 16 September 1982.
4. See Ian Adamson, *The Identity of Ulster: the land, the language and the people* (Belfast, 1982), *passim*.
5. *The Irish Times*, 9 January 1981.
6. *Report of a Committee to consider Police Interrogation Procedures in Northern Ireland*, Cmnd 7497, 1979.
7. Stephen Greer, *Fortnight* no. 198, October 1983: see the counter-argument put by Edgar Graham in the same issue.
8. *Anglo-Irish Joint Studies. Joint Report and Studies*, Cmnd 8414, 1981, p. 33.
9. See, for example, Conor O'Clery, *The Irish Times*, 18 July 1979.
10. T. K. Whitaker, *The Irish Times*, 25 March 1982.
11. William Whitaker, HC Deb., 846, 46, 13 November 1972.
12. Oliver MacDonagh quoted in Michael McKinley, 'The Ulster Question as an International Issue', unpublished PhD thesis, Australian National University, Canberra, 1982, p. 369.
13. See, for example, leading articles on 18 March 1980 and 27 October 1980.
14. See the contributions of Bernard Crick, Maurice Vile and Patrick Keatinge in D. Rea (ed.), *Political Co-operation in Divided Societies*. (Gill and Macmillan, 1982). See, too, Charles F. Carter, 'Permutations of Government', *Administration*, Winter 1972, pp. 50–57.

Bibliography

(An asterisk indicates that the book has been published in paperback)

1. Historical background

The two standard textbooks are J. C. Beckett, *The Making of Modern Ireland, 1603–1923** (Faber, 1969), and F. S. L. Lyons, *Ireland Since the Famine** (Fontana, 1973). Both are scholarly and detailed, and the latter has the advantage that it discusses contemporary problems. Another good general introduction is Nicholas Mansergh, *The Irish Question, 1840–1921** (Unwin, 1965), valuable because it examines English attitudes to the Irish question in a European context.

The books for the specialist are Richard Rose, *Governing Without Consensus* (Faber, 1971) and Ian Budge and Cornelius O'Leary, *Belfast: Approach to Crisis*, (Macmillan, 1973). The former draws widely on contemporary political science literature to give the most rounded picture of Northern Ireland politics. The latter has a very good political history of Belfast, but its second half is for the specialist interested in the quantitative approach to political studies.

A third category covers books of a more propagandist nature. The best known – and best written – is Conor Cruise O'Brien, *States of Ireland** (Hutchinson, 1972, 2nd edn, Panther, 1974). Its particular value lies in its demythologisation – it is a 'revisionist' account of Irish history. Another work in this category is Brian Farrell (ed.), *The Irish Parliamentary Tradition* (Gill and Macmillan, 1973): it stresses that the violent side of Irish history has been given too much airing by examining a durable parliamentary tradition over eight centuries. Finally, within this third category, we can make a crude division between 'Nationalist' and 'Unionist' studies. Frank Gallagher, *The Indivisible Island*, (Gollancz, 1957) and Michael Farrell, *Northern Ireland: The Orange State** (Pluto Press, 1976) belong to the former group. Farrell's study has the merit that it is based on much detailed research of the period 1918–75 but is 'not an impartial book' and is written 'from an anti-imperialist and socialist standpoint'. Unionist views are represented by two more scholarly studies: M. W. Heslinga, *The Irish Border as a Cultural Divide** (Van Gorcum, 1972) and A. T. Q. Stewart, *The Narrow*

Ground (Faber, 1977). Heslinga is a Dutch geographer who sees the Ulster problem in the context of regionalism within the British Isles. Stewart is an Irish historian who attempts to redress the balance on the contemporary literature on the Ulster crisis; he believes (rightly) that the propaganda battle is being won by those who write on behalf of the minority population.

2. Political institutions

The best introduction for the general reader of the devolved system of government in Northern Ireland is Martin Wallace, *Northern Ireland: 50 Years of Self-Government*, (David and Charles, 1971); it is clear, concise and balanced, although slightly dated. One useful book which fills the gap is John Oliver, *Working at Stormont* (Institute of Public Administration, 1978). Oliver was a senior civil servant who had worked at Stormont for over forty years. His memoirs betray a certain complacency but are valuable as the thoughts of an insider and as one who was very closely involved in constitutional developments after the introduction of direct rule in 1972.

A more academic account of political institutions is the aptly-titled work of a constitutional lawyer, Clair Palley, *The Evolution Disintegration and Possible Reconstruction of the Northern Ireland Constitution* (Barry Rose Publishers, 1973). Another academic study, R. J. Lawrence, *The Government of Northern Ireland* (Oxford University Press, 1965) is more concerned with public finance and the public services. A more dated, but valuable work is Nicholas Mansergh, *The Government of Northern Ireland: A Study in Devolution* (Allen and Unwin, 1936). A complementary volume which brings the narrative up to date is W. D. Birrell and A. Murie, *Policy and Government in Northern Ireland: Lessons of Devolution* (Gill and Macmillan, 1980). It is rather dull reading for the general reader but essential for the student of public administration.

3. Society and culture

Two books are recommended as useful introductions to the nature of a divided society: D. P. Barritt and C. F. Carter, *The Northern Ireland Problem** (Oxford, 1962, rev. edn Oxford University Press, 1972) is a pioneering work written by two Quakers. The social anthropologist Rosemary Harris has written an excellent study of a border village, based on observer-participation, *Prejudice and Tolerance in Ulster* (Manchester University Press, 1972). It is for the specialist reader and, although her field-work was undertaken before the present 'Troubles' began, it is full of sharp insight and common sense. Another useful specialised study, examining a specific problem, the history of education legislation in Northern Ireland, is Donald Akenson, *Education and Enmity*, (David and Charles, 1973).

Two books which examine the community divide from each side of the sectarian barriers are Eamonn McCann, *War and an Irish Town* (Penguin,

1974, rev. edn. Pluto Press, 1980) and Ron Weiner, *The Rape and Plunder of the Shankill*, (published by the author, Belfast, 1975). McCann writes graphically of life in Derry's Catholic Bogside area and of his own involvement in the civil rights campaign; Weiner writes vividly of urban renewal (and destruction) in the Protestant Shankill area of Belfast.

Finally, the memoirs of a retired civil servant, Patrick Shea, *Voices and the Sound of Drums: An Irish Autobiography* (Blackstaff Press, 1981), may more properly belong to the previous section. But these delightful memoirs of 'a cuckoo in the nest' tell us a good deal more about Ulster society than a library of social science textbooks.

4. Political parties

There is no specific published study of opposition parties in Northern Ireland between 1921 and 1969. The two best introductions are for the specialist: Ian McAllister, *The Northern Ireland Social Democratic and Labour Party* (Macmillan, 1977) and E. Rumpf and A. C. Hepburn, *Nationalism and Socialism in twentieth-century Ireland* (Liverpool University Press, 1977). McAllister is concerned with a party which was born only in 1970 but he writes a good account of nationalist politics in the preceding years. Rumpf and Hepburn are primarily concerned with politics in the Republic, although they have one good chapter examining Ulster politics, especially the role of the NILP.

The Unionist party is much better served by academics. The best historical introduction is the work of a sociologist, Peter Gibbon, *The Origins of Ulster Unionism* (Manchester University Press, 1975). It is stimulating and provocative but is not to be recommended to the general reader. A more conventional academic exercise is John F. Harbinson, *The Ulster Unionist Party 1882–1973: its Development and Organisation** (Blackstaff Press, 1973). As its title suggests, this is more an examination of the organisation of the party than of its ideology. An historical narrative covering the first twenty years of Northern Ireland, Patrick Buckland, *The Factory of Grievances* (Gill and Macmillan, 1979), is a sympathetic account of Lord Craigavon's premiership. The author has exhausted the resources of the Public Records Office of Northern Ireland, and his book can be used as a valuable source for the period. Another historical narrative, D. W. Miller, *Queen's Rebels* (Gill and Macmillan, 1978), is a highly readable and fascinating account of the concept of 'conditional loyalism'.

Two former Prime Ministers have written their memoirs, Terence O'Neill, *Autobiography* (Hart-Davis, 1972), and A. B. D. Faulkner, *Memoirs of a Statesman* (Weidenfeld and Nicholson, 1978). These are valuable, contemporary accounts of the Unionist Party in turmoil.

5. The economy
Again, there is no specific book-length study of the Northern Ireland economy or of Anglo-Irish relations. Garret Fitzgerald, an economist and leader of Fine Gael, the major opposition party in the Irish Republic, examines these questions in *Towards a New Ireland** (Temple Smith, 1972) and republished since (Torc, 1973) in paperback. A. H. Birch makes many useful references to these matters in his *Political Integration and Disintegration in the British Isles** (Allen and Unwin, 1977). A sophisticated Marxist analysis, *The State in Northern Ireland*, by Paul Bew, Peter Gibbon and Henry Patterson (Manchester University Press, 1979) makes extensive use of recently released State Papers and is probably the most detailed study of the question. It is a stimulating book but it cannot be recommended to the general reader.

6. Political developments since 1968
Although there has been a massive literature published on Northern Ireland since 1968, there is no one compact text-book which adequately explains the bewildering turn of events. Many of the books already referred to cover different facets of the contemporary problem. But there are only three recently published books concerned specifically with the past decade. The first by V. Magowan and R. Deutsch, *Chronology of Events in Northern Ireland, 1968-74** (Blackstaff Press, 1973, 1974 and 1975) is a massive three-volume document which gives a day-by-day account of life in Northern Ireland in these years. The second, *Northern Ireland: A Time of Choice** by Richard Rose, (Macmillan, 1976), covers the major political developments between 1968 and 1975, but is not of the same rigorous standards as his *Governing Without Consensus*. A third, *Northern Ireland: A Political Directory, 1968-83*, by W. D. Flackes (Ariel Books, 1983) is a more compact and more topical revision of Deutsch and Magowan. It analyses the contribution of personalities and organisations, the effects of election results, the systems of government and the security system over the past decade.

The external dimensions of the question have begun to merit attention. Two studies from Dublin are important. Patrick Keatinge, *A Place Among The Nations: Issues of Irish Foreign Policy* (Dublin, Institute of Public Administration, 1978), is as its title suggests, concerned with wider questions, but it is a useful source for examining the Irish Republic's growing awareness of the Ulster problem. More relevant are the memoirs of a former British Ambassador to Ireland who has 'gone native', John Peck, *Dublin From Downing Street* (Gill and Macmillan, 1978). A more speculative treatment can be found in D. Rea (ed.), *Political Co-operation In Divided Societies* (Gill and Macmillan, 1982). It contains some very valuable essays on Sovereignty, Federalism and Anglo-Irish Relations. Finally, a good 'insider' account is that of James Downey, *Them and Us: Britain, Ireland and the Northern Question, 1969–1982* (Dublin, Ward River Press, 1983).

Much of the most interesting recent work is to be found in academic journals and political weeklies. A careful reading of the footnotes to each chapter will give you some idea of the breadth of the writing on Northern Ireland. For a more detailed study of this breadth you could consult John Darby *Conflict in Northern Ireland: The Development of a Polarised Community* (Gill and Macmillan, 1977), which is, essentially, an extended bibliography of the vast material on the subject.

Index

(Northern Ireland is abbreviated NI)